Pub Scene

This publication is designed to provide accurate and authoritative information in regard to the subject matter covered. It is sold on the understanding
that the Publisher is not engaged in rendering professional services. If professional advice or other expert assistance is required, the services of a
competent professional should be sought.

Other Wiley Editorial Offices

John Wiley & Sons Inc., 111 River Street, Hoboken, NJ 07030, USA

Jossey-Bass, 989 Market Street, San Francisco, CA 94103-1741, USA

Wiley-VCH Verlag GmbH, Boschstr. 12, D-69469 Weinheim, Germany

John Wiley & Sons Australia Ltd, 42 McDougall Street, Milton,
    Queensland 4064, Australia

John Wiley & Sons (Asia) Pte Ltd, 2 Clementi Loop #02-01,
    Jin Xing Distripark, Singapore 129809

John Wiley & Sons Canada Ltd, 22 Worcester Road, Etobicoke, Ontario,
    Canada M9W 1L1

ISBN-13 978 0 470 01809 5 (HB)
ISBN-10 0 470 01809 7 (HB)

Layouts by Ian Lambot
Printed and bound by Conti Tipocolor, Italy

Pub Scene

Jane Peyton

Additional photography **Helen Peyton** and **Robert Howard**

Series Designer **Liz Sephton**

contents

Executive Commissioning Editor: Helen Castle
Development Editor: Mariangela Palazzi-Williams
Content Editor: Louise Porter
Publishing Assistant: Calver Lezama

Preface

In *Pub Scene* I use the term 'pub' generically to describe café-bars, taverns, bierkellers, hotels, saloons, beer gardens or any similar establishment to visit for an alcoholic drink. I also use 'beer' as a generic term, sometimes using it interchangeably with ale and lager. Despite communal drinking in a specific building – i.e. a pub – being a worldwide practice, I mainly refer to British examples when I discuss pub trends; lack of space prevented me from including the view from other countries.

It was difficult making a final choice of pubs to feature because there are so many brilliant options. In the end I went for places that I really enjoy and that are photogenic. The selection is English-centric, but that is because there is an embarrassment of riches in England. So to all the fantastic pubs in the rest of the UK and world that were left out, I look forward sometime to writing *Encyclopaedia Pub Scene*.

Photo Credits

Cover: © Helen Peyton
pp 1, 5 (br), 9 (t), 10 (cr), 13, 14 (cr), 16-17, 20-31, 32 (tr), 33-35, 66-69, 78-85, 86 (tl), 87 (tr), 92-103, 170-171, 174-179, 186-189, © Robert Howard; pp 2-3, 202-207 © Ron McCulloch; pp 4 (tl), 10 (tl), 32 (br), 36-53, 54 (tl), 55-63, 64 (b), 65, 88-91, 128-133, 166-169, 190-195 © Helen Peyton; pp 4 (br), 70-71, 112-117 © Anson Smart; pp 5 (tl), 118-119, 134-141 © Paul Gosney; pp 5 (bl), 142-143, 146-151 © Geoff Mason; pp 8, 97 © Shepherd Neame; pp 9 (cl) © Granada Television; pp 11 (b) © Ross Honeysett; pp 12 © Mark Townsend; pp 14 (tl), 15 © National Trust; pp 54 (tr, cr & br) © Christina Seyferth; pp 59, 64 (t) © Tony Harman; pp 74-77 © Jonny Valian; pp 82, 86 (b), 87 (b) © Johan Seutens; pp 104-105, 109-111 © Camera and Design; pp 106-108 © David Webb; pp 122-127 © Stuart Thomas; pp 152-159 © Gordon Biersch; pp 160-165 © Richard Leeney; pp 180-185, 196-201, 213 © Greg Humphrey; pp 208-209 © Jane Peyton

key: t top; b below; c centre; l left; r right

Pub Scene is dedicated to Tony Harman of Maple Leaf Images, Skipton, with thanks for being such an ace photo developer and generous camera benefactor.

Thank you to all the people who helped me to compile *Pub Scene*. Particular thanks to Roisin Rock, polyglot extraordinaire, for her translation skills and endless cuppas at Café RoRo. Grateful thanks to The Pitfield Beer Shop in London for permitting me to photograph a fraction of their extensive stock of domestic and international beer. I highly recommend the Pitfield Brewery's

Acknowledgements

Eco Warrior, East Kent Goldings and Black Eagle organic bottled brews which refreshed the parts that cups of tea could not reach as I was writing this book. At Wiley-Academy, many thanks to Helen Castle who asked me to write *Pub Scene*, and to Mariangela Palazzi-Williams, Famida Rasheed and Louise Porter; for post-production, to Ian Lambot, and to Abigail Grater and Julia Dawson for copy-editing.

I am indebted to the designers and photographers who generously gave me free use of their photographs – Emily Dent of designLSM (who was also endlessly patient with my questions and requests) and Greg Humphrey for The Catcher in the Rye and Salt House; Stuart Thomas for The Harrow; Keith Galbraith and Geoff Mason for Galbraith's Alehouse; Johan Seutens and Fred Dericks for De Ultieme Hallucinatie; Cameron Bayfield and Paul Gosney for Newport Arms Hotel; Ross Honeysett and Mark Landini for Cruise Bar; Christina Seyferth for Löwenbräukeller; Mel Cook and Ron McCulloch for the White Horse Hotel; Kylie Fitt at SJB Interiors for Woolwich Pier Hotel and the Colombian Hotel; Denise Starbird, Mike Curtis and Mark Stevens for Gordon Biersch; Jennie Madden and Mark Townsend for The Bell and Drift; Shepherd Neame for Manor Farm Barn, The Harrow and the Chelsea Flower Show garden; Oliver Peyton, Rochelle Cohen and Richard Leeney for Mash; David Webb and Camera and Design for JD Wetherspoon; the National Trust for the George Inn; Granada TV for the Rovers Return.

I was fortunate in being able to consult several design experts about subjects related to contemporary and historical pub design, so thank you very much to Simon Hudson of designLSM, Robert Thomas of Remarkable Restaurants Group, and Martin Godden of Shepherd Neame.

And many thanks to all architects, designers, PR executives and pub landlords who helped me at short notice and were extremely gracious – including Mark Stevens of Architecture & Light, Tim Trapp of Trapp Associates; Clare Pope and Zoe Springett at Edwards Harvey; Kate Clifford at Isis PR; Ashley Halliday at JD Wetherspoon; Joanne Looby at Guinness; Sarah Downing, Manager of the unique Prince Alfred in London; and Marie-Louise Wong, licensee of Liverpool's stunning Philharmonic Dining Rooms.

Finally to Helen Peyton, my sister, who did additional photography and makes photo-shoots such fun even when it means getting up at 2 am to travel to our destination – bottoms up!

'There is nothing which has yet been contrived by man, by which so much happiness is produced as by a good tavern or inn.'
Dr Samuel Johnson (1709–84)

Cheers

Imagine life without the pub. Where would we go to meet our friends, commemorate special occasions, flirt with prospective lovers, gossip, escape to, put the world to rights? Pubs perform a role that is more than just a dispenser of drinks. Take away a pub, particularly in a village, and the heart of that community is damaged. Most societies where alcohol is legal have pub-like places for people to drink and socialise in, variously known as bars, hotels,

Introduction

cafés, brasseries, bodegas, lodges, inns, saloons, taverns, beer halls and shebeens. Commenting on the inimitable qualities of the public house, Martin Godden, pub designer at English brewer Shepherd Neame, says: *'You often see people of very different backgrounds, generations and ethnic origins all meeting together, debating, chatting and socialising. There are not many places where such a diverse mix of people can feel comfortable together and socially interact.'*

This book is not about beer, but without the nectar of Ninkasi, Ishtar Siduri and Isis (respectively the Sumerian, Babylonian and Egyptian goddesses of beer) the pub, as we know it, would not exist. So, as a primer on that truly global

Above: Chelsea Flower Show 2005, London.
The garden that won top prize at Chelsea Flower Show 2005 was recreated in 2006 at The New Flying Horse, Wye, Kent, – a pub owned by Shepherd Neame.

Left: Chelsea Flower Show 2005, London.
Brewer Shepherd Neame supplied the pub sign in Chelsea Flower Show's prize-winning garden 'A Soldier's Dream of Blighty', based on what World War II soldiers missed about Britain when they served overseas.

Above **Falstaff, Brussels.** Art Nouveau facade of the Victor Horta-designed Brussels café bar.

Above **The Rovers Return, Coronation Street.** Mirroring real life, in the soap opera *Coronation Street*, the Rovers Return pub is the centre of the community.

beverage – bier, öl, cerveja, olut, biera, ölu, birra, bière, cerveza – and how it became a progenitor of the public house, the following text is a gallop through a few historical highlights.

Picture the history of beer as a dartboard and Sumeria, Southern Mesopotamia, in what is now modern-day Iraq, as the bullseye. On a clay tablet dated to the 3ʳᵈ millennium BC, people are depicted drinking from a communal vessel – the earliest evidence of beer. Then in the epic poem *Gilgamesh*, the world's oldest written story dating back 4,000 years, beer is mentioned several times. As the Sumerian civilisation faded, the Babylonians ascended to become the regional superpower in politics and brewing – they allegedly produced 20 different types of beer for domestic consumption and export. For ancient Egyptians beer was a vital commodity with such status that a hieroglyphic was created for 'brewer'. In addition to being revered as a drink, it was also an effective medicine for treating numerous ailments and dressing wounds because, although unknown to medics at the time, grain used in the brewing process contained Streptomyces bacteria that produce the antibiotic tetracycline.

By now the art of brewing and drinking of beer was firmly established in the Mediterranean – long before viticulture came to dominate the region. For a balanced diet the Greek writer Sophocles (who lived c. 496–406 BC) recommended 'bread, meat, green vegetables and *zythos* [beer]'. And as for the question 'What did the Romans ever do for us?' – well, as their empire spread across Europe, so did knowledge of beer. Armies of occupation constantly on the move needed somewhere for rest and relaxation, so along roads they built *mansiones* and *diversoria* and in towns *tabernae*, pit stops that sold food, wine and the local brew – in effect, nascent pubs. Northern Europe in particular became very partial to beer, and after the fall of the Roman Empire, as dominant tribes began to fill the power vacuum and invade other lands, they took their culture and practices with them. But it was with the advent of Christianity across much of the continent that beer became a fundamental aspect of society. Monks built breweries in monasteries, and established inns to provide shelter, food and drink to pilgrims visiting holy sites. Once beer became a regular component of the diet (being a liquid version of bread), villagers – usually women – took over the responsibility of brewing using pooled resources. It was always a sociable drink with special brews produced to mark events such as weddings (the term 'bridal' is a corruption of 'bride-ale') and church festivals ('yuletide' actually means 'ale-tide').

Left: **The Guildford Arms, Edinburgh.** A smart new dining room overlooks the main bar of The Guildford Arms in Edinburgh and attracts a clientele that might not normally have patronised this pub.

Mud In Your Eye

The evolution of the English pub shadows the country's development from an agrarian society to a largely urban, post-industrialised country where people have significant disposable income. In medieval England, as the population increased and industry expanded, spreading pollution with it, water was not always safe to drink so beer was the alternative. From the 13th century, alehouses became a permanent feature in towns and villages – places of rest and relaxation for the poor. They were usually in the homes of the brewer, sometimes with simple tables and benches that shared the cramped space with the private dwelling. In large urban areas, the rich typically were much better catered for, with taverns selling expensive imported wine and decent food. Though not sumptuously furnished, taverns were more elaborate than their basic poorer cousins that were licensed to sell beer only, and they attracted a higher class of drunk who discussed politics, talked business, and caroused. They were places for a convivial night out, locations for professionals to hold meetings, and they offered facilities for the great and the good to entertain in. The decline of taverns as a specific type of hostelry came about towards the end of the 18th century when their monopoly to sell wine was revoked – coffee houses poached custom and alehouses were permitted to offer more than just beer.

Above: **Greenwich, Brussels.** Chess devotees meet nightly to play at the Greenwich bar in Brussels.

Another strand of pub DNA is the coaching inn – a descendant of the 12th-century inns established by monks as shelter for pilgrims. As people and goods had more reason to travel, particularly after the Industrial Revolution irrevocably changed society, there was a requirement for locations at which to stop, feed, water and rest the horses and passengers. Coaching inns along transport routes offered food, drink, shelter and stables. Some of them were upgraded alehouses, others grand, purpose-built structures, several storeys high, often with a central courtyard for carriages to drive into, surrounded by galleries off which bedrooms were situated. These inns were not just used by travellers: they became venues for entertainment – minstrels sang, plays were performed and freak shows attracted customers. They hosted sporting events, balls, lectures, civic business and were a valuable asset of the community. With the construction of railways from 1825, coaching inns lost custom and those that did not close down were transformed into hotels or continued as pubs to service the villages and towns that had grown up around them.

Bottoms Up

By the early 19th century, the British Government was determined to halt the ruinous effect that Madame Geneva, or gin, had on the urban poor. Ever since King William III had encouraged its consumption in the late 17th century by removing restrictions on distilling spirits, an underclass appeared to be permanently drunk. Some workers' wages were even partially paid in gin. Rampant alcohol abuse with all its associated vices, increased crime and its deleterious effect on health had terrible consequences for society. In 1830, the Beer Act was passed allowing anyone to open a beer house on payment of a token fee. The intention was for the price of beer to drop below that of gin so people would turn away from the evil spirit to the more benign brew. Thousands of beer houses were set up but the new law did nothing to arrest the epidemic of drunkenness, and almost forty years after the law was enacted, the Government repealed it and most seedy drinking dens closed. During that period, however, a type of pub had emerged that is still familiar today. Nicknamed 'gin palaces', they were extravagant fantasies, opulently furnished, luxuriously decorated and run as legitimate businesses. Often situated on street corners near slum areas, the intention was to attract people who wanted to escape, if only for the time it took to swallow a glass of porter, from their dreadful living conditions. *'They transported the public to Sybaris for a night or two,'* says Robert Thomas, from the Remarkable Restaurants Group, specialists in restoring grand old boozers.

At first gin palaces were one-room establishments, but soon partitioned spaces became the norm, grouped round a central bar island. This meant that people of different classes could drink in the same pub but not be seen by each other, as snob-screens, frosted glass and separate entrances offered privacy. A boom in pub building in the last decades of the 19th century coincided with

Below: Cruise Bar, Sydney. Landini Associates designed Sydney's fashionable Cruise Bar and its slick beer pumps.

the strongest economy Britain had ever known. Inside, elaborate woodwork, etched and painted mirrors and plate glass, moulded walls and ceilings, pillars, and ceramic tiles became a hallmark of Victorian pubs; and outside, imposing Renaissance and Baroque facades, or whatever grand architectural statement that could be dreamt up, proved irresistible to customers regardless of class.

By c. 1910, expensive gin palaces were no longer being constructed. Instead, a wistful romantic version of Olde England – a combination of rustic, medieval, and mock Tudor, also known as 'Brewer's Tudor' – spread as a popular pub style in town and country late into the 1930s. Pub building was halted during World War II, and in the post-war era, austerity measures dictated that new pubs were of a basic style: in comparison to the glory days only a few decades earlier, they were little more than functional boxes. Gone was the fun and fantasy vision of the Victorian and Edwardian period of pub design.

Pubs have always been commercial entities that owners modify if it means a boost in profits. From the 1970s, the pace of refurbishment increased with original layouts destroyed, often to make one large room, and fake heritage bestowed with old photos and 'antiques'. In the 1980s, theme-concepts such as the ersatz Irish pubs that spread in a green wave to cities all over the world became the trend, followed in the 1990s by what Martin Godden refers to as "Supermarket Pubs", *'where it did not matter which part of the country you were in, a certain brand of pub environment would be exactly the same'.*

A major influence on recent pub design has been 'girl power' – a phenomenon that is sometimes called 'the feminisation of leisure'. Increased equality, spending power and consumption of alcohol by women has had a significant impact on pub culture. Simon Hudson of designLSM sums up the key aspects of making a female-friendly pub: *'open up picture windows to let passers-by see inside – no secrets; lighten up the design; offer coffee, tea and a bigger choice of juices; remove old-fashioned hand-pulled ales and replace with continental lagers via chrome fonts; top-notch ventilation; merchandise the bar to best display a wider range; replace beer-sodden carpets with boarded floors or new carpet with contemporary designs; use floral decorations; improve loos 500%.'* And appealing to women makes commercial sense because, as Simon points out, *'most men don't care anywhere near as much as women about the design of a pub. So if it is attractive to females, business will improve*

Above: **The Bell, Tanworth-in-Arden, West Midlands.** An essential village pub at the heart of the community houses the Post Office, a deli-catessen and a coffee shop, as well as a smart restaurant and hotel rooms — everything a pub should be and more.

Left: **Drift, Birmingham.** Bespoke leather furniture in the corner of a stylish pub.

Right: **Sun Inn, Barnes, London.** A modern pastime in an antique pub.

Below: **Sun Inn, Barnes, London.** Regency-style chairs with jolly sun-motif backrests

and the men will still go in there anyway.' A chain of urban pubs called All Bar One aimed at female drinkers was the first in 1994 to capitalise on this huge untapped market and since then, the majority of new or refurbished pubs and bars have used the design language, staffing techniques (friendly, young, good-looking) and merchandise that appeal to women.

Many people rue the disappearance of traditional boozers all over the country, as they are renovated, cleaned up, and turned into stylish, design-led, lounge-like hangouts. Others argue that without modernisation, pubs often lose custom and may close down altogether. But for lovers of pub heritage there is a sobering fact: according to a 2003 report by the Campaign for Real Ale (CAMRA), guardians of the National Inventory of Pub Interiors of Outstanding Historic Interest, less than 4% of approximately 60,000 public houses in the UK have retained historically significant features.

Down the Hatch

When designing today's public houses, architects and designers take into account the Three Gs – Great Building, Great People, Great Products. For Martin Godden, the Three Gs can also be described as the theatre of retail, with the analogy of the pub as a stage show: *'The building and interior represents a set; staff and customers the actors; and products, food and drink etc. the script. For the pub to succeed, all three elements need to be right. From the pub designer's point of view, I can clearly influence the former. We are now seeing more and more that a Hellenistic approach to pub design is necessary in order*

*to be highly effective, i.e. product range, target audience and staff
characteristics should all be considered when designing or altering a pub.'*

Bearing in mind one must generalise when discussing a pub customer,
depending on mood, people have different reasons for and expectations of
'going down the pub'. For fun and celebration they are likely to head for a
bustling town centre location – a large open-plan layout, possibly with music
and discounted drinks offers. Conversely, couples out for a quiet evening may
choose a suburban or country pub with an intimate lounge. Unconsciously what
patrons look for includes the emotional factors of familiarity, security, and
feelings of comfort, recognition and belonging. Lifestyle is also an issue and a
person's self-perception will be reflected by their choice of pub. In the past few
years, a section of the general public with substantial spending power has
become accustomed to good interior design. Makeover TV programmes and
magazines in particular have widely driven the assumption that if a person is
going to spend money on their social life, they expect to do it in attractive
surroundings. But because people want different things from pubs, there is no
one design model that appeals to everyone all the time. What customers widely
respond to currently in furnishings is sofas, dramatic lighting fixtures, artwork,
and fresh flowers; and in product, choice of real beer and continental lagers,
cocktails, a wide choice of wine, and imaginative food menus.

According to Simon Hudson, the biggest current trend is the
*'"Contemporary Local" – a pub that serves the local community, keeps the good
things about "tradition" yet has all the requirements of the age, i.e. it is clean,
airy, has non-smoking areas, all-day trading, smart design – a place where you
want to be seen.'* For two examples of this format, check out The Catcher in the
Rye and Salt House, both designed by Simon's company designLSM.

Martin Godden believes that *'we are moving much more towards individual
and unique pub environments, and away from branded chain pubs. The use of
natural and raw materials is now commonplace, which in a way reflects society's
more environmentally friendly attitude. There is a shift to pubs with separate
areas, rather than a big open space, which is, of course, going back to Victorian
days. In the past, these divisions were class-based, but in the future I feel they
could be more based on people's needs and feelings.'* The Harrow and Manor
Farm Barn, designed by Martin for Shepherd Neame, illustrate these points
perfectly.

This book contains a selection of pubs designed or refurbished in a range
of styles from various periods. The common denominator is that they all look

great and are popular destinations, used and appreciated by customers for a variety of reasons. With the exception of the heritage listed locations and their protected status, such as the Crown Liquor Saloon in Belfast and The Philharmonic Dining Rooms in Liverpool, in ten years' time the British and Australian featured pubs may have been altered again to reflect modern tastes – proving that the pub will never go out of fashion, it just evolves to suit the market.

Finally, a pub quiz. Who described their perfect pub as:

a) 'One that is open'

b) 'A tiny freehouse in the village where I live. The food is great, the company excellent and peace and quiet are "on-tap"'

c) 'An idyllic country pub, which has evolved through the years, where each postcard behind the bar, or piece of singed ceiling, or scratch on the floor, has a story to tell, and where the roaring fire in winter and baffled light in the early summer evening all add to the unique and welcoming atmosphere. The eccentric landlord, diverse range of customers, and worn-out sofas add to the ambience – it is the kind of place where, once settled in, you could quite happily stay until the early hours'

Was it: Simon Hudson; Martin Godden; or Jane Peyton's next-door neighbour Frank?

Answers: a) Frank   b) Simon Hudson   c) Martin Godden

Below: The George Inn, Southwark, London.
This atmospheric inn was a well-known coaching terminus and dates to 1676. It was mentioned in Charles Dickens' *Little Dorrit*.

YE OLDE MASTERPIECE
Classic Pubs

Masterpiece is a fitting noun to describe the pubs in this section. The architects who designed them let their imaginations soar and produced works of art worthy of veneration. Whilst diverse in appearance, what they have in common is that someone – whether the pub's owner, the brewery, or the architect – considered the provision of a beautifully designed environment for drinking and mingling to be of such value that they were willing to spend money to realise their vision. There were various reasons for owning an impressive public house: for a start, they made good business sense by attracting new custom or enticing customers away from competitors; they were a high-profile outlet for a brewery's product; they encouraged civic pride; they were status symbols and fashion statements. These marvellous pubs recognised the fundamental role of alcohol by providing a stunning backdrop for the ceremony of socialising.

Ye Olde Masterpiece

The pubs in the following pages have historic interiors that attract visitors who come to admire the craftsmanship, experience the atmosphere and continue the tradition of previous generations by enjoying the surroundings. Look in city tourist guides and these pubs are all featured – sometimes they are the sole reason for a person to visit a particular place.

A la Mort Subite is a Brussels stalwart noted for its laid-back atmosphere. Many other Belgian café-bars are Art Nouveau or medieval-looking, so A la Mort Subite, dating from 1928, stands out for its rococo décor. With its dimly lit long rectangular shape, high ceiling, lines of wooden tables and benches, one can disappear into the characterful interior and sit contentedly for hours.

Another Brussels spot that attracts visitors with an eye for architecture is L'Archiduc, the very definition of va va voom. L'Archiduc was built in 1937 in the fashionable, "Streamline" Moderne style and immediately became *une maison des rendez-vous d'amour* where wooing couples could snuggle up in booths and gaze at each other. Today people are more likely to be gazing at the gorgeous curvaceous interior, because outside certain esteemed hotels and cocktail bars, it is not easy to find such beautifully preserved Art Deco.

If London were a Walt Disney theme park, The Black Friar would be its pub because it is decorated with jolly friars in bas-relief and mosaics, with naughty wooden devils to tempt them. The pub occupies land on which a medieval Dominican monastery formerly stood. It was built in 1905 and showcased the hands-on skills of the Arts and Crafts ideology – a movement supported by architects, craftsmen, and artists who protested against the industrialisation of society. Apart from The Black Friar, there are no surviving complete Arts and Crafts pubs, so it is a priceless fragment of Britain's heritage.

'Survivor' also describes the Crown Liquor Saloon in Belfast – owned by the National Trust and one of the most incredible pubs in the world. With its eye-catching ornate décor both inside and out, its drinking boxes and its original gas lighting fixtures still used for illumination, it is special indeed. But this is no museum, it is enormously popular and lively with customers from near and far who come to admire and have a drink in such a singular setting.

An unexpected delight is concealed behind a discrete facade in Dublin's premier shopping and entertainment quarter. Davy Byrnes is the epitome of Art Deco glamour and unlike any other pub. The current owner is the son of the landlord who made the decision in 1941 to change the décor from that of a traditional Irish boozer to the height of sophistication. Good move, because its drop-dead chic interior differentiated it from all others and it attracted a higher-spending clientele that continues to frequent the pub today.

To look at it, one would never know Löwenbräukeller was rebuilt in the 1950s after suffering a direct hit from World War II Allied bombs. The refurbishment restored the vast 19th-century beer hall to its medieval castle style. With its barrel-vaulted ceilings and heavy marble pillars, this traditional bierkeller ambience is a great draw and it remains a popular element in Munich's beer heritage.

Liverpool has much to boast about in its architectural landscape and this includes the Philharmonic Dining Rooms commissioned in 1900 by powerful local brewer Robert Cain. A city ranked as one of the busiest ports in the world deserved a lavish public house such as the Philharmonic to serve the numerous wealthy merchants, and showcase the status of Cain.

Robert Cain also paid for the construction of The Vines. The city-centre pub built in 1907 has some wonderful Arts and Crafts features and a stunning brass bar counter. Like the Philharmonic, it performed the dual role of showing off Cain's good taste and his beer, and providing a smart destination for Liverpudlians to spend their money in.

In the unwritten rules of gin palace design there is no such phrase as 'too flamboyant', and the Warrington Hotel in London supports that. From the outside, with its magnificent tiled and mosaic entrance, to inside, where Art Nouveau bordello meets Italian Renaissance gentlemen's club with a few 1960s murals thrown in, the Warrington Hotel kept 'em and still keeps 'em coming to marvel at the décor. And that all adds to profits, which of course is why pubs are in business.

A la Mort Subite

Designer unknown

Location: Brussels, Belgium
Completion Date: 1928

Throw away your watch because time seems to stop in A la Mort Subite, where the décor and atmosphere transport customers to a previous era. Sit down at a table, order a drink and suddenly life slows down, guaranteed.

The name 'A la Mort Subite' (translated as 'sudden death') refers to a dice game played at La Cour Royale, a bar owned in 1910 by Théophile Vossen. Customers threw dice during work breaks and, when it was time to return to the grind, a game of sudden death was thrown. In 1928 Vossen opened the establishment featured here and named it after those last-minute games. Today his great-grandsons run the bar and little has changed.

It is easy to see why A la Mort Subite is a Brussels institution. Walk through the glass entrance and you find yourself in an atmospheric, dimly lit retreat where you can sit for hours and read, write, chat or daydream. The long oblong room with wooden tables, chairs and benches has a high ceiling supported by several Corinthian columns. Along the walls are huge arched gilt mirrors with gilded plasterwork surrounds, and between them stencilled floral discs and pilasters on which lamps with flower-bud-like shades are fixed. The colour scheme is burnt sienna and turmeric – what some might describe as nicotine – creating a warm ambience. At the far end, a glamorous double staircase leads up to a balcony and smaller room illuminated through a stained-glass skylight.

Behind the bar is a wall of glasses in a number of shapes and sizes: each beer is served in its own unique glass. Chimay, for instance, comes in a bowl-like vessel on a stem and Duvel in a curvaceous tulip-shaped receptacle designed to release the aroma of the brew. For fans of Belgian beers, this is sampling heaven with a tempting selection including Trappist, Abbey, and Mort Subite, a style of Gueuze named after the bar.

Picture this scene. A mysterious, good-looking stranger sits on a bench against the wall. On the table is a goblet containing amber, slightly sparkling sour and sweet beer, a plate of cheese with mustard on the side and a newspaper. An emptied glass later, the customer looks at the menu etched on a mirror, attracts the attention of the waiter and orders another drink. Golden ale with a thick white head is brought to the table. Mmmm, Westmalle – creamy and softly bitter with a fruity aroma. So who is the lucky person? Make haste to Brussels and it could be you.

Opposite: A la Mort Subite, Brussels, Belgium. Looking down on this perfect Belgian café bar from the balcony

Below: A la Mort Subite, Brussels, Belgium. Grimbergen is a popular Abbey beer so these glasses will not be empty for long

	A La Mort Subite
Address	7 rue Montagne-aux-Herbes-Potagères, 1000 Brussels, Belgium
Telephone	+32 (0)2 513 1318
Opening hours	Mon-Sat 11am to 1am Sun 12.30pm to 1am
Design style	Rococo
Drinks	A wide selection of Belgian beers, wine, champagne
Music	None
Special features	Snack food and light meals

Opposite: A la Mort Subite, Brussels, Belgium.
Corinthian style columns support the ceiling of this
large café bar

Above: A la Mort Subite, Brussels, Belgium. A
stained-glass panel of the King of Beer and a
happy horseman, the logo of Mort Subite Gueuze
beer, enjoying a draught

Left: A la Mort Subite, Brussels, Belgium.
Mirror, mirror on the wall, what is the tastiest
Belgian beer of all?

Right: **A la Mort Subite, Brussels, Belgium.** Huge arched mirrors create infinite reflections

Below: **A la Mort Subite, Brussels, Belgium.**
Serving up a glass of Grimbergen Abbey beer

Left: **A la Mort Subite, Brussels, Belgium.**
Gueuze, faro and lambic beer named after the bar

Right: A la Mort Subite, Brussels, Belgium.
A very contented cat

L'Archiduc

Designer unknown

Location: Brussels, Belgium
Completion Date: 1937

If De Ultieme Hallucinatie with its elegant Art Nouveau interior is a *grande dame*, and A la Mort Subite with its rococo styling a playful roué, then L'Archiduc is a soigné and wildly sophisticated bright young thing. In a land-locked city, this bar with its elegant streamlined interior is the nearest thing the Bruxelloises have to an Art Deco cruise-liner. As soon as one enters through a fancy glass and wrought iron lobby, straight lines are abandoned in favour of oh-so-sexy curvaceous forms. L'Archiduc comprises an oval-shaped space on two levels and no matter where one looks, curves are queen.

At the room's focus are two central columns girded by chrome plating, sentries to a grand piano, on which great entertainers, including Nat 'King' Cole, have played. It is a well-used keyboard because live sessions titled 'Jazz After Shopping' and 'Round About Five' are played on Saturday and Sunday afternoons respectively from September to May.

Velvet-upholstered banquettes line the perimeter walls. When L'Archiduc opened in 1937, these were separated into booths by wooden screens and the establishment was known as *une maison des rendez-vous d'amour,* a discreet location perfect for a private romance. Today, the seating is open-plan, with barrel-like chairs or z-shaped chrome high stools up against an undulating walnut bar, but there is still a feeling of intimacy borne of the interior curvature and low-level balcony hugging the periphery of the room. The colour scheme is muted marine green and cream for walls and ceiling, with soft furnishings in air-force blue, carmine and mustard patterned velvet. During the day natural light filters through pastel-coloured stained-glass windows and at night the bar is dimly lit by chrome Art Deco wall-light fixtures specially designed in the 1980s for L'Archiduc.

So understated is the elegance of L'Archiduc that after the initial impact and admiration of the setting, one can concentrate on having a lovely drink dispensed from a compact and good-looking wood, chrome and marble bar – curved, of course – from which a serpentine silver beer pump rears up. Belgium's beer superstars are on the menu, including Westmalle, Chimay, Orval and others, and an impressive selection of whisky and cognac is always in-house for those who prefer the 'water of life'.

Above the ornate entrance is the letter 'A', fashioned in swirling wrought iron. It stands for Alice, after the bar's first owner, as well as Archiduc and Amour. In such gorgeous surroundings, with languorous lounge music playing on the sound system, it's easy to fall in love.

Above: **L'Archiduc, Brussels, Belgium.** The wrought iron letter 'A' above the entry stands for Archiduc, Alice and Amour

Opposite: **L'Archiduc, Brussels, Belgium.** The balcony resembles the bridge of an Art Deco cruise-liner, while the sexy curves give this room 'va va voom'

L'Archiduc

Address	6 rue Antoine Dansaert, 1000 Brussels, Belgium
Telephone	+32 (0)2 512 0652
Opening hours	Daily 4pm to 6am
Design style	Art Deco
Drinks	Belgian and international beer, wine, champagne, cocktails and a wide selection of whisky and cognac
Music	Recorded jazz and lounge music
Special features	Live jazz at the weekends

YE OLDE MASTERPIECE

Opposite: **L'Archiduc, Brussels, Belgium.** On the balcony looking towards the ornate entryway

Above: **L'Archiduc, Brussels, Belgium.** Shadows from a decorative wrought iron doorway

Left: **L'Archiduc, Brussels, Belgium.** Walking from the street into an elegant Art Deco time capsule

Above: **L'Archiduc, Brussels, Belgium.** Behind
a discrete facade lies Brussels' perfect Art Deco
maison des rendez-vous d'amour

Opposite: **L'Archiduc, Brussels, Belgium.**
Columns flank the piano, making it the central
focus of the room

Below: **L'Archiduc, Brussels, Belgium.** A
serpentine chrome beer pump rears up from
the bar

Right: **L'Archiduc, Brussels, Belgium.** A
chrome handrail curves around the wooden bar

The Black Friar

H. Fuller-Clark and Henry Poole

Location: London, UK
Completion Date: 1905 and 1924

Thank you, thank you to all the people who vociferously campaigned in the 1960s and saved The Black Friar from demolition. Imagine if the developers had won and destroyed one of the most singular pubs in existence, denying visitors who come from all over the world the joy of gazing at the spectacular Arts and Crafts styling.

Even from outside, The Black Friar looks like no other building – a tall, narrow triangular structure marooned between busy roads and a railway bridge. The statue of a black friar above one door and a mosaic depicting his fellow brothers carrying fish and wine above another entrance are visual clues to the history of the site: a Dominican monastery was situated there from the 13th century until 1538 when it was pulled down during the Dissolution of the Monasteries. The monks wore black robes, hence the nickname.

For an unforgettable first impression of the interior, enter the pub through the side door under the trees. Spin around and take it all in – green, red, brown and yellow marble walls, elaborate mosaics, copper plaques and bas-reliefs of fat, jolly monks. Astonishing! Over the bar a frieze entitled 'Tomorrow Will Be Friday' depicts friars collecting fish and eels for the following day when eating meat was forbidden for Catholics. Above the fireplace the brothers sing and play musical instruments in a frieze called 'Carols', and on another one, 'Saturday Afternoon', they gather fruit.

And there is more. Walk through the archway into an incredible marble-lined room with a barrel ceiling covered in intricately patterned golden-hued mosaics. Atop four columns sit black marble devils, each carrying out an artistic pastime – reading, playing an accordion, painting and acting. While the devils amuse themselves, some of the monks toil, weighed down by yokes from which hang lampshades. All work and no play makes black friars dull boys, evidenced by the rather stern epigrams spelled out in mosaic : 'Industry is All', 'Silence is Golden', 'Finery is Foolery'. Then the devils have their say with 'Seize Occasion' and 'Don't Advertise It, Tell A Gossip'. But look a little closer: the monks are being tongue-in-cheek with their proclamations – one is boozing and one is snoozing.

Light filters into The Black Friar through a wall of small-paned windows and stained-glass panels that give it an ecclesiastical feel. The front part of the pub with its own entrance is, compared with the lavish décor elsewhere, plain and unremarkable. As these two sections were once divided, the unadorned room was likely a taproom for the *hoi polloi* and the decorative saloon for gentlemen, a common distinction in the class-conscious early 20th century.

Fittingly for such a special place, The Black Friar has a Grade II* English Heritage listing that will preserve this priceless gem for the future.

Above: The Black Friar, London, UK. The pub is an island marooned by road and rail, with mosaic monks above the entrance to remind its patrons to eat fish on Fridays

Opposite: The Black Friar, London, UK. The intricately designed mosaic ceiling in the snug — this room was originally the luncheon bar

The Black Friar

Address	174 Queen Victoria Street, Blackfriars, London EC4V 4EG, UK
Telephone	+44 (0)20 7236 5474
Opening hours	Mon-Sat 11am to 11pm Sun 12 noon to 10.30pm
Design style	Arts and Crafts
Drinks	Cask ales, international lagers, wine, regular pub drinks
Music	None
Special features	Pub grub and bar snacks

Left: The Black Friar, London, UK. Monks in a copper bas-relief entitled 'Carols'

Below: The Black Friar, London, UK. Another copper panel, this time on a marble column

Right: The Black Friar, London, UK. Looking from the saloon into the snug

Right: **The Black Friar, London, UK.** An accordion-playing little devil, sits on a cornice beneath the mosaic ceiling of the snug, itself a stupendous example of the skill of Edwardian craftsmen

Below: **The Black Friar, London, UK.** The whole interior of the pub is an Arts and Crafts showcase

Café Royal

Robert Peterson and J. Macintyre Henry

Location: Edinburgh, UK
Completion Date: 1862, 1893 and 1901

How to spend an unforgettable day out in Edinburgh: breakfast at Valvona & Crolla in the *caffè* of that peerless Italian deli; lunch on the best sausage and mash in the land at Monster Mash; then take afternoon tea in the Palm Court of the Balmoral Hotel where home-made shortbread melts in the mouth. In between those pit stops, stroll around the World Heritage capital city looking up at the architecture; and marvel at just how grand 19th-century Scottish banks could be in the Royal Bank of Scotland's banking hall on St Andrew Square before the sun goes over the yard-arm and it is time for a drink. Where else would crown the day but the Café Royal?

Without it being intimidating or unwelcoming (quite the opposite), the Café Royal is the type of place that subconsciously makes the chin lift up, shoulders go back, and posture straighten. Cole Porter would undoubtedly have described it as 'swellegant' and it is hard to ignore the sophisticated surroundings. Yet this is an establishment for everyone whether they like to drink cask ale, good wine or a cup of coffee in a room with a view. And what a splendid prospect it has. The public bar is called the Circle Bar, though semi-circular is more accurate. It is a large, uncluttered room with crescent-shaped booths that allow customers a largely unrestricted panorama. A central island bar has a mahogany gantry and several Olympic torch-style lamps on top of brass fluted Corinthian columns that surface from the highly polished counter.

Down one wall is a series of irreplaceable Doulton Lambeth faïence wall panels that depict inventors and scientists at the moment of their discovery: for instance William Caxton, Benjamin Franklin, Louis Daguerre and James Watt. If the 'Science and Nature' questions in Trivial Pursuit were formerly a no-go area, then after a visit to the Café Royal that will no longer be the case. 'The father of electrical engineering? Easy, that's Michael Faraday.'

Behind a carved walnut screen with bevelled mirrors is the Oyster Bar, an elegant wood-panelled restaurant with its own display of art in the handsome stained-glass windows that depict strapping men playing popular sports – tennis, rugby, fishing, and five others.

Nowadays this must-see pub is protected by a Grade A heritage listing, but that was not always the case. In the 1960s, retail chain FW Woolworth attempted to buy the property and demolish it to provide access for their adjacent Princes Street store. Thankfully the plans were rejected. For lovers of Victoriana, it is impossible not to feel *Schadenfreude*: the Café Royal is now in its third century as an Edinburgh institution, whilst the local Woolworth's has ceased trading.

Above: **Café Royal, Edinburgh, UK.** One of Edinburgh's jewels in a quiet haven off Princes Street

Opposite: **Café Royal, Edinburgh, UK.** The wooden screen at the far end of the room separates the Circle Bar from the Oyster Bar

Café Royal

Address	17-19 West Register Street, Edinburgh EH2 2AA, UK
Telephone	+44 (0)131 556 4124
Opening hours	Mon-Wed 11am to 11pm Thur 11am to 12 midnight Fri-Sat 12 noon to 1am Sun 12.30pm to 11pm
Design style	French Second Empire
Drinks	Cask ales, international lagers, extensive wine list, regular pub drinks
Music	Recorded
Special features	A la carte menu in the Oyster Bar and bar snacks

Above: **Café Royal, Edinburgh, UK.** A selection
of fine Scottish beers attracts lovers of real ale

Opposite: **Café Royal, Edinburgh, UK.** A
panoramic view of the Circle Bar

Right: **Café Royal, Edinburgh, UK.** The servery counter in the Oyster Bar, with celebrated stained-glass windows as a backdrop

Far right: **Café Royal, Edinburgh, UK.** Leather banquettes line the curved wall of the Circle Bar

Left: **Café Royal, Edinburgh, UK.** Priceless hand-painted Doulton ceramic murals line the inner wall of the Circle Bar

Above: **Café Royal, Edinburgh, UK.** The stained-glass windows in the Oyster Bar depict men occupied in various sporting activities

Below: **Café Royal, Edinburgh, UK.** A view towards the entrance of the Circle Bar

Crown Liquor Saloon

Patrick Flanagan

Location: Belfast, Northern Ireland, UK
Completion Date: 1885

'Masterpiece' is an overused word but in this case it is accurate. In a beauty pageant of Victorian gin palaces, the Crown is certainly queen. Such is the priceless decoration of this one-of-a-kind watering hole that it has a Grade A heritage listing and is owned by the National Trust.

What is so special about it? Well, for a start, it is remarkable that this dowager has survived intact because it is situated directly opposite the Europa Hotel that had the unfortunate experience of being bombed several times during the late-20th-century terrorist campaign. And then there is the facade covered by polychromatic ceramic tiles and decorated by classical columns and pilasters, portholes and stained-glass windows. Step over the mosaic entry floor and into another era with original gaslights (still working and used every day), and along one wall 10 incredible snugs, or drinking boxes – carved wood and painted glass units that in class-conscious Victorian times screened drinkers from prying eyes. Today they remain much in demand for secret rendezvous, confidential conversations, quiet lunches and for the novelty value of having a private room within a public house.

Spectacular as the snugs are, the rest of the pub is equally notable with something new to notice during each visit. The bar servery is a long red granite-topped fixture faced with yellow ceramic patterned tiles and divided by mahogany mirrored screens. A heated brass footrest runs along its base. Behind the bar is a hardwood cabinet that contains huge wooden casks with polished brass taps, and which is decorated with coloured mosaic words

Opposite: **Crown Liquor Saloon, Belfast, Northern Ireland.** When customers ring the bell in one of the drinking boxes it registers on this panel

Above: **Crown Liquor Saloon, Belfast, Northern Ireland.** The unique facade is lined with eye-catching polychromatic ceramic tiles around the pub's entrance

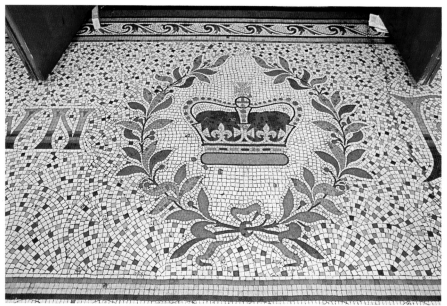

Left: **Crown Liquor Saloon, Belfast, Northern Ireland.** There can be no doubt what name is represented in the entrance mosaic

Crown Liquor Saloon

Address	46 Great Victoria Street, Belfast BT2 7BA, Northern Ireland, UK
Telephone	+44 (0)28 9027 9901
Opening hours	Mon-Sat 11.30am to 12 midnight Sun 12.30pm to 10pm
Design style	Victorian Gin Palace
Drinks	Ales, international lagers, wine, regular pub drinks
Music	Recorded
Special features	Bar snacks downstairs and a full menu in the restaurant upstairs

Left: **Crown Liquor Saloon, Belfast, Northern Ireland.** Mosaics, tiles, stained glass and wooden carvings — there is no shortage of decorative details to admire

proclaiming the pub's former distinction as a 'High Class Whiskey Importer'. The ceiling is decorated with yellow, gold and red plasterwork and supported by carved wooden columns with Corinthian capitals; the walls are brocaded; pilasters are tiled; windows are stained; and everywhere you look glass is painted or etched with shells, fleurs-de-lys, fairies and pineapples (this fruit symbolises hospitality). 'More is more' is the concept here, and it works beautifully – the pub is constantly busy with admiring customers.

For some, the Crown Liquor Saloon reminds them of a Baroque church interior – particularly with the stained glass, the mosaic floor, and the snugs that distinctly resemble confessional boxes. Perhaps this is to be expected: Belfast experienced a boom in church construction following the Emancipation of the Catholics in Northern Ireland in the early 19th century, and the skilled craftsmen who created the pub in 1885 were Italians moonlighting from building houses of worship.

But despite its status as a heritage property this is no museum, and it works efficiently as a vibrant business that attracts visitors from all over the world. The sheer scale and artistry of the decorative interior and exterior is stunning and encourages people to talk; and that is, to use the Irish phrase, the start of a good *craic* – what all pubs aspire to.

Above: **Crown Liquor Saloon, Belfast, Northern Ireland.** A painted glass panel detail on the door of one of the drinking boxes

Below: **Crown Liquor Saloon, Belfast, Northern Ireland.** Old wooden casks with brass taps extend the length of the bar

Above: **Crown Liquor Saloon, Belfast, Northern Ireland.** Italian craftsmen created the interiors, including the elaborately carved drinking boxes or 'snugs'

Right: **Crown Liquor Saloon, Belfast, Northern Ireland.** Walk through the front door and you are greeted with this glorious interior

Davy Byrnes

Original designer unknown; extended by Cantell & Crowley

Location: Dublin, Ireland
Completion Date: 1942 and 1987

'Never judge a book by its cover,' warns the proverb, and this is especially true of a discreet facade just off Dublin's Grafton Street that conceals the divine Art Deco Davy Byrnes pub. It's a walloping surprise to walk in off the street and see the exquisite hand-painted floral wooden and stained-glass ceiling, black wall-hugging bench seats and booths, lily-like brass light fixtures and undulating bar servery faced with dozens of black dots that on close examination turn out to be the bottoms of champagne bottles. Gorgeous does not describe it.

And that's not all. Walk further into the pub – it stretches back and back – onto a red carpet heralding another section with a curvilinear bar servery and mirrored curved walls. Wooden panels and frames are trimmed with black plastic swirling shapes; a polished wood column is crowned with a modern brass sculpture of flying doves and above it, a stained-glass cupola filters multi-coloured light into the room. There is no clue that this back area of the pub was added to the original 1942 Art Deco front 45 years later. It melds seamlessly and enhances the glamour of this singular spot. Utterly va va voom!

Casual visitors on 16 June each year may wonder why hundreds of people squeeze into the premises and order a gorgonzola and mustard sandwich and glass of burgundy. They are on the Bloomsday Trail, doing exactly what Leopold Bloom in James Joyce's *Ulysses* did on that day. Joyce was a regular at Davy Byrnes and wrote of his character Bloom: *'He entered Davy Byrnes. Moral pub. He doesn't chat. Stands a drink now and then. But in a leap year once in four. Cashed a cheque for me once.'* Bloom's thoughts about the pub – *'Nice quiet bar. Nice piece of wood in that counter. Nicely planed. Like the way it curves'* – referred to the pre-Art Deco interior when it was an unremarkable Irish boozer.

Literature is not the only art at Davy Byrnes: notable murals, paintings and sculptures are also on display. But it is through writing that the pub is most celebrated because it was a haunt of a number of great Irish authors. It is also the final stop on Dublin's celebrated Literary Pub Crawl, which is led by two actors who introduce the writers and act out scenes from their work. And with an eye to future Irish giants of letters, the Doran family, owners of the pub since 1942, sponsor the Davy Byrnes Irish Writing Award.

Dublin has some unforgettable pubs, but none looks like Davy Byrnes and that makes it even more special.

Above: **Davy Byrnes, Dublin, Ireland.** Ornate light fixtures in the shape of lilies hang from a floral hand-painted ceiling

Opposite: **Davy Byrnes, Dublin, Ireland.** Light streams through a stained-glass cupola to the rear of the pub, on to a dramatic red carpet that brings extra glamour to a sophisticated interior design

	Davy Byrnes
Address	21 Duke Street, Dublin 2, Ireland
Telephone	+353 (0)1 677 5217
Opening hours	Mon-Wed 11am to 11.30pm Thur-Fri 11am to 12.30am Sat 10.30am to 12.30am Sun 12.30pm to 11pm
Design style	Art Deco
Drinks	Irish ale, international lagers, wines, regular pub drinks
Music	Recorded
Special features	A la carte menu and bar snacks; particularly noted for seafood

Above: Davy Byrnes, Dublin, Ireland. The extension built in 1987 enhances the original Art Deco pub

Above: Davy Byrnes, Dublin, Ireland. The bar base is decorated with the bottoms of dozens of champagne bottles

Above: Davy Byrnes, Dublin, Ireland. Mirrors reflect light and make the narrow room look bigger

Right: **Davy Byrnes, Dublin, Ireland.** Murals painted in the 1940s by Cecil Ffrench Salkeld

Below: **Davy Byrnes, Dublin, Ireland.** Splendid Art Deco styling seen from the pub entrance

Löwenbräukeller

Albert Schmidt and Friedrich von Thiersch

Location: Munich, Germany
Completion Date: 1883-98, rebuilt 1950

Ever walked into a pub and been unable to decide where to sit? Well, at Löwenbräukeller multiply that indecision because it is a vast beer hall with a warren of rooms on three storeys – the banquet hall alone has 2,000 seats. In total, over 4,100 guests can be seated inside and in the beer garden.

When Löwenbräukeller opened in 1883, it offered a deluxe service like none other in Munich – that is, napkins and tablecloths. Moreover, customers were not required, as in other places, to bring their own glasses and utensils and clear up after themselves. It started off as a big draw for locals and it still is, with a clientele made up of Müncheners as well as tourists. It has become a stalwart of the city's hospitality, hosting enormous banquets, weddings, and other special events. But its aged patina is deceptive: the structure was rebuilt in 1950 after being reduced to rubble by Allied bombs during World War II, and restored again in the 1980s when the banqueting hall and associated rooms were destroyed by fire. Rather than have a rampant lion as the logo, maybe a phoenix would be more accurate.

Beer connoisseurs might want to visit Löwenbräukeller in March when the annual tapping of the new season Triumphator takes place. Maybe this strong beer is to Müncheners what spinach is to Popeye, because during the celebration it is traditional for beefy chaps to try to lift a stone weighing over 230 kilograms, attempting to emulate Hans Steyrer, the 19th-century Bavarian Hercules who, legend suggests, used his middle finger alone to raise the rock.

If the wind is blowing in the direction of Löwenbräukeller, visitors will smell the unmistakable aroma of brewing beer from the mighty Löwenbräu brewery just next door – with such proximity, the tipple is fresh indeed. The keller's main public bar room, known as Bräustüberl, has a vaulted ceiling, Romanesque columns, brass chandeliers, and resembles a medieval church. Several smaller areas decorated in a variety of styles and colours fan out from this central space and are used for drinking, dining, or special parties.

It is a carnivore's paradise, with whole spit-roast ox regularly prepared in the beer garden and an extensive menu of hearty Munich delicacies such as the special platter of duck, pork knuckle, brisket, chicken, sausages, sauerkraut, dumpling, coleslaw, and potato salad. Such a feast, served inside the baronial splendour of the bierkeller or out in the shady garden, needs to be accompanied by a Löwenbräu beer – perhaps a stein of Schwarze-Weisse, Dunkel or one of the brews made specifically for Oktoberfest. What a magical process that turns simple ingredients – hops, barley, water, and yeast – into such delicious refreshment.

Above: **Löwenbräukeller, Munich, Germany.** A vast edifice, this Munich landmark dominates a busy intersection

Opposite: **Löwenbräukeller, Munich, Germany.** The cavernous Bräustüberl, with its vaulted ceiling and Romanesque columns, resembles a medieval church

Löwenbräukeller

Address	Nymphenburgerstraße 2, Am Stiglmaierplatz, 80335 Munich, Germany
Telephone	+49 (0)89 526 021
Opening hours	Daily 10am to 12 midnight
Design style	Medieval Castle
Drinks	A selection of Löwenbräu beers
Music	Recorded
Special features	A la carte menu of Bavarian specialities and beer garden snacks

Opposite: **Löwenbräukeller, Munich, Germany.** The fancy chandeliers in the Pilsstube room are adorned with metal plaques painted with scenes of the brewing process

Below: **Löwenbräukeller, Munich, Germany.** A weekly treat for carnivores, when a whole ox is roasted

Above: **Löwenbräukeller, Munich, Germany.** Images of hops, barley and brewing implements are etched on the vaulted ceiling of this function room

Right: **Löwenbräukeller, Munich, Germany.** One side room, the Jägerstube, is lit by a spooky chandelier — the figure of a brewer with antlers instead of legs

Right: **Löwenbräukeller, Munich, Germany.** The huge banqueting hall can seat 2000 people

The Philharmonic
Dining Rooms

Walter Thomas

Location: Liverpool, UK
Completion Date: 1900

Words are inadequate to describe the utterly fabulous interior of the Philharmonic Dining Rooms. England's most spectacular pub is named after the Philharmonic Hall opposite, and was built in 1900 to cater to concertgoers and wealthy locals who lived in the area. As society was still segregated by class at that time, the front bar, or Vault, was rather plain and for the use of domestic staff and other working people, while the extraordinary Lobby Bar, and dining, smoking and billiard rooms were for gentlefolk.

Typical of gin palaces, the lavish décor begins on the outside with a set of striking Art Nouveau wrought-iron gates at the main entrance that lead customers along a magic carpet of mosaic into the Lobby Bar. As film directors sometimes say, 'this is the money shot' – magnificent woodwork, Corinthian pillars, stained glass, ceramic wall tiles and a circular hardwood bar faced with brightly coloured mosaic. At this instant there are two types of visitor – those standing looking around with jaws dropping at the architecture and those with jaws dropping at the great choice of cask ales. Since becoming the licensee in the year 2000, Marie-Louise Wong has transformed the Phil, as it is universally known, from a pub with one indifferent beer, to a destination for real-aleophiles, presenting up to ten notable brews at any time and earning a slot in *The Good Beer Guide*.

A treasure such as the Phil needs regular maintenance and since 2000 a good deal of restoration has been undertaken with the greatest of care and scrutiny given that the structure is protected by a Grade II* English Heritage listing. This refurbishment has ensured that the pub looks as good as it possibly can. One superficial change is the billiard room, now called the Grande Lounge, where food is served at lunchtime. It retains original wood panelling inlaid with brass bas-reliefs of fish and birds of prey and a ceiling-height plaster frieze adorned by caryatids and other comely ladies.

It is not unusual to see large groups gathered outside the gates waiting for opening time so the visitors, many of whom come from all over the world, can view for themselves the uniqueness of this much-loved landmark. Marie-Louise Wong sums up the Phil perfectly: when asked why people should visit, she replied, *'People should come for the same reasons they go to Venice, Rome or Paris – to be awed by its splendour, to be stunned by the craftsmanship required to build it, to be astonished by its very survival. They should also come to have a pint of perfect ale, a great meal and to enjoy the humour, the warmth and pantomime that is Liverpool at its best.'*

When Liverpool-born former Beatle John Lennon was asked what the negative aspects of fame were, he allegedly replied: *'Not being able to have a drink at the Phil.'*

Opposite: **The Philharmonic Dining Rooms, Liverpool, UK.** The pub's superb interior was created by craftsmen who fitted out luxury liners

Below: **The Philharmonic Dining Rooms, Liverpool, UK.** The pub is a Liverpool landmark that attracts visitors from all over the world

The Philharmonic Dining Rooms

Address	36 Hope Street, Liverpool L1 9BX, UK
Telephone	+44 (0)151 707 2837
Opening hours	Daily 12 noon to 12 midnight
Design style	Extravagant Arts and Crafts
Drinks	Guest cask ales, lagers, wines, regular pub drinks
Music	Recorded
Special features	Extensive menu of pub grub favourites

YE OLDE MASTERPIECE

Opposite: **The Philharmonic Dining Rooms, Liverpool, UK.** It is no wonder that the 'Phil' is known as England's most lavish pub

Below: **The Philharmonic Dining Rooms, Liverpool, UK.** A changing selection of excellent guest ales guarantees the pub's inclusion in *The Good Food Guide*

Above: **The Philharmonic Dining Rooms, Liverpool, UK.** A wood panelled corridor leads from the bar to the Grande Lounge past rooms originally used for private dining and smoking

Left: **The Philharmonic Dining Rooms, Liverpool, UK.** An ornate corner of the Lobby Bar

Left: **The Philharmonic Dining Rooms, Liverpool, UK.** Even the men's loos are unforgettable

Above: **The Philharmonic Dining Rooms, Liverpool, UK.** St Cecilia, the patron saint of music, bestows blessings on the Royal Liverpool Philharmonic Orchestra based in a concert hall opposite the pub

Right: **The Philharmonic Dining Rooms, Liverpool, UK.** The cavernous wood-panelled Grande Lounge was formerly a billiard room with stained-glass skylights

Right: **The Philharmonic Dining Rooms, Liverpool, UK.** Flamboyant Art Nouveau wrought-iron gates herald the treasure inside

The Vines

Walter Thomas

Location: Liverpool, UK
Completion Date: 1906-7

Like its sister up the road, the Philharmonic Dining Rooms, this glorious pub was designed by architect Walter Thomas. He was commissioned by local brewer Robert Cain to transform an existing Victorian public house into something worthy of Liverpool. The city, 700 years old in 1907, was arguably at the zenith of its importance as a commercial centre and one of the British Empire's leading ports, so grand pubs like this were built to recognise Liverpool's exalted status and soak up the disposable income of its citizens.

No escape from wood at The Vines – in wall panels, columns, screens, arches and other ornamental features. Decorative plasterwork comes a close second with swags, leaves, pot-bellied putti in a frieze that encircles the Smoke Room and gilt-horned devils on the ceiling of the public bar who can be blamed for urging customers to 'go on, have another one'.

Spare a thought for the cleaners who daily polish the endless brass rails and the incredible bar bottom that resembles the hull of wooden ship. Don't leave behind any fingerprints! Turn around from this bar and a copper and marble fireplace flanked with two gorgeous goddesses in the form of wooden caryatids greets the eye. Back-to-back with the Ancient Greek beauties is an even more ornate fireplace, in the Smoke Room. This one is framed by mahogany Corinthian columns that enclose a beaten-copper fire-surround and above it a bas-relief of Viking ships. The Vikings knew Liverpool and the city's name might even derive from Old Norse words meaning 'muddy creek'. Seating in the Smoke Room is compartmentalised into bays by narrow wooden screens and each recess has a bell push. This suggests that at one time these alcoves might have been more like private drinking booths, with bells used to summon table service.

The grandest room in the house is now used for parties and live entertainment. The Heritage Suite has a stained-glass cupola, crystal chandeliers, Corinthian pilasters, Victorian portraits hanging on the walls, and an enormous mahogany fireplace, above which is a huge gilt-framed mirror. Around the room heavy wooden panels are carved with feathers and swags, and brass lampstands bear light shades in the shape of flower buds. Whereas the other rooms in the pub are light and fun, this one is stern. It was formerly the billiard room and its imposing décor demonstrates how important the game was in gentlemen's pubs.

With its striking Baroque and Arts and Crafts interior, The Vines richly deserves its Grade II* English Heritage listing.

Above: **The Vines, Liverpool, UK.** Local nicknames for the pub include the Grapes and Clock — inside, a golden satyr peers mischievously from the ceiling of the Lounge Bar

Opposite: **The Vines, Liverpool, UK.** Fine mahogany panelling and stained glass in the Lounge Bar

The Vines

Address	81-89 Lime Street, Liverpool L1 1JQ, UK
Telephone	+44 (0)151 709 3977
Opening hours	Sun-Thur 12 noon to 12.30am Fri-Sat 12 noon to 2 am
Design style	Baroque meets Arts and Crafts
Drinks	Regular pub drinks
Music	Recorded
Special features	Regular special events including live music

Above: The Vines, Liverpool, UK. Spare a thought for the cleaners who have to polish the magnificent brass bar and fittings each morning

Right: The Vines, Liverpool, UK. Viking ships in full sail adorn a bas-relief above the fireplace in the Smoke Room

Above: **The Vines, Liverpool, UK.** Plasterwork cherubs cavort in a frieze that encircles the wall of the Smoke Room

Below: **The Vines, Liverpool, UK.** Art Nouveau glamour girls flank another of the pub's fireplaces

Left: **The Vines, Liverpool, UK.** One of the caryatids that support the mahogany and beaten copper fireplace

Warrington Hotel

Designer unknown

Location: London, UK
Completion Date: 1858, refurbished c. 1900

From the first moment of clapping eyes on the incredible faïence pillars, tilework, mosaic floor and gas lamps that adorn the Warrington Hotel entrance, one can see this is no ordinary pub. And the reason the overture is so extravagant is a big tease for the symphony inside. Choose the right-hand door and – *ooh la la!* – is it a bordello or a gentlemen's club? A wall-painting of semi-naked glamour girls that dates from the mid-1960s suggests the former; whereas heavy wood-panelling and richly patterned William Morris-style wallpaper evoke the latter. Neither is correct, although rumours that the hotel was once a brothel persist. Perhaps Maida Vale's pre-World War I reputation as an area where the mistresses of rich men were domiciled fuelled whispers of a Warrington Hotel bagnio.

Refurbished at the height of Britain's gin palace popularity, the Warrington Hotel was situated in an upmarket residential part of London and it made sense to establish an opulent public house that appealed to wealthy locals and their domestic staff. Art Nouveau was a popular style of the time, but to be on the safe side, and appeal perhaps to a more conservative patron, familiar decorative motifs of the Victorian era were included – for instance, a grand staircase and Renaissance archways supported by Corinthian marble pillars. This combination offers plenty to look at and provides great conversation openers between today's customers.

The bar servery – surely one of the most memorable anywhere – is semi-circular with a marble top and splendid ornamented oak base. So far so Victorian, but take a step backwards and raise the gaze. Camp does not begin to describe the fancy carousel-shaped fixture with cherubs that prop up an orange mural of swinging sixties chicks who look like the stars of a hairspray commercial. Hanging from it are ten bell-shaped lampshades on chains, illuminating the unit in such a way that from a distance it resembles the Mothership from *Close Encounters of the Third Kind*. This pub has to be seen. Elsewhere there is fine stained, painted and etched glass, two simpler rooms with separate entrances originally used by less affluent customers, and an opulent first-floor dining room that is now a Thai restaurant.

As for drinks, the choice of wine by the glass or bottle is excellent, and beer-drinkers will find much to please with Fuller's, Shepherd Neame, Young's and guest ales. In fine weather the leafy beer garden might well tempt drinkers outside. Perhaps they are minimalists – why else turn away from this remarkable interior?

Above: Warrington Hotel, London, UK. The main entrance is every bit as gorgeous as the interior and incorporates a welcoming mosaic that has endured over a century of footfall

Opposite: Warrington Hotel, London, UK. The pub features one of the fanciest bar designs anywhere

Warrington Hotel

Address	93 Warrington Crescent, Maida Vale, London W9 1EH, UK
Telephone	+44 (0)20 7286 2929
Opening hours	Mon-Sat 11am to 11pm Sun 12 noon to 10.30pm
Design style	Gin Palace and Art Nouveau mix
Drinks	Real ales, international lagers, wines, regular pub drinks
Music	Recorded
Special features	Thai restaurant on the first floor

Above: Warrington Hotel, London, UK. A Renaissance-style arcade in an Art Nouveau-tinged Gin Palace

Right: Warrington Hotel, London, UK. A grand staircase leads to the Thai restaurant on the first floor

Right: Warrington Hotel, London, UK. The voluptuous marble-top counter incorporates richly carved panels and pilasters

Above: Warrington Hotel, London, UK. The maidens' hairstyles date the mural above the bar to the mid-1960s

Below: Warrington Hotel, London, UK. There is no end of glorious colour here, with a floral ceiling, stained glass, gilding and murals of 'girls with the sun in their hair'

THE BUILDERS ARMS
Converted and New Build Pubs

Consider the evolution of pubs and it becomes apparent that they are promiscuous makeover subjects. Even the most perfectly preserved gin palaces have undergone some restoration or alteration that modernises or improves the services they offer. Pubs will never go out of fashion because their owners can give them a face-lift to respond to current trends. Redesigning a pub is like re-branding it, leading to additional business and often a new clientele. Increasingly buildings that had a former use are being converted to pubs, some so successfully that they look as though they have always been there. And as the estate agents say, it's location, location, location – the right pub in the right place at the right time will attract custom.

The Builders Arms

Proof of this slogan is the fantastic success of the Colombian Hotel, a former bank in Darlinghurst, Sydney's gay enclave. SJB Interiors transformed it into a glamorous pub that opened just as the city hosted the Gay Games in 2002. Situated on Darlinghurst's main street, it has been packed out ever since.

Another ex-bank, now a pub, is The Counting House, situated in the City, London's financial district. It's an imposing Victorian interior that in the past would have proclaimed the bank's wealth and status. Today it looks as though it has always been a pub because the architects did such a brilliant design job; they were presented with a City Heritage Award for sensitive refurbishment. The ornate wooden island bar in particular, although constructed as recently as 1998, looks a century older and perfectly corresponds with the distinguished interior. It has proved a successful location for a pub with an extensive food menu and it's constantly busy, especially at lunchtime.

Brussels is an Art Nouveau fanatic's nirvana with some of the world's most spectacular buildings embellished in that decorative style. One such example designed in 1904 by architect Paul Hamesse is discreet on the outside, but inside so fancy that words do it no justice. Until 1981 this was a private house, after which it opened as a restaurant and tavern called De Ultieme Hallucinatie. To reach the tavern, constructed as an understated conservatory in the rear garden, means a walk through the extraordinary house, and it is the association with such a unique artefact of the Art Nouveau movement that attracts customers for a drink.

Guess what Ireland's number one tourist attraction is … it's the Guinness Storehouse, situated in an early 20th-century warehouse, refurbished in 2000, that tells the story of Dublin's inimitable stout. Inside the building is a 30-metre-high atrium in the shape of a giant glass, and on top of it, like the creamy head of a pint of Guinness, is the glass Gravity Bar, a circular design that offers an unrivalled panorama of the city. It's unforgettable and has people gasping as they exit the lift and see the view.

Manor Farm Barn is an award-winning pub in an 18th- century threshing barn. This is another brilliantly realised design that looks as though it has been there for decades but dates only from 2002. Shepherd Neame, the brewery that owns the pub, is England's oldest brewer and so tradition runs deep. Manor Farm Barn is a great example of a conversion that perfectly harmonises with and enhances its environment.

Not all distinguished pubs are immune from decay. The Salisbury in North London was designed by a Victorian property developer to show off the immediate neighbourhood that he also built. Late in the 20th century, the pub's opulence diminished through neglect. That is until the Remarkable Restaurants Group, specialists in restoring faded boozers to their original elegance, bought it. Once again it is a splendid-looking place and most impressively refurbished.

Champion at converting existing buildings into pubs is JD Wetherspoon, with hundreds of properties in its portfolio, dozens of which are in former churches, cinemas, and theatres, and others in new-build structures. Each pub is different – there is no corporate look, and the company commissions several architecture practices to work on locations in the ever-growing chain. The pubs featured here show a range of 'looks' in buildings that were once working men's clubs, furniture stores, and a railway recruitment office, as well as ground-up constructions.

One glittering example of how the refurbishment of a pub can reposition it in the market is the Woolwich Pier Hotel. Despite being on Sydney's prestigious North Shore, the classic Victorian hotel had a rough, tough reputation and clientele. Ever since the pub was made-over in slick resort style with the addition of a chic beer garden, cocktail lounge and bistro all looking out over the world-famous harbour, it has been celebrated as a destination to flock to for smart nosh and tipple.

The pubs featured in this section are a diverse selection of beauteous boozers in Australia, Belgium, England, and Ireland.

The Colombian Hotel

SJB Interiors

Location: Sydney, Australia
Completion Date: 2002

Familiar with the lyrics to Barry Manilow's composition 'Copacabana'? The Colombian Hotel with its South American-influenced décor is that song come to life, especially when one looks around at the clientele of this enormously popular mixed gay and straight pub and remembers the central characters are Lola, a showgirl, Tony, a handsome barman, and Rico, a smooth lothario.

To create one of Sydney's most grooving pubs, SJB Interiors took an Art Deco former bank on the main street in Darlinghurst and transformed it into a two-storey pub, lounge and dance club in a cocktail of two parts Latin American tropical, one part Native Indian tribal iconography and a dash of glamour graffiti. On the ground floor, the asphalt jungle meets the rainforest in a lush palm-tree-and-toucan mural; stools are covered in patterned vinyl snakeskin that could be anacondas in another life; and geometric ironbark wood high tables have a hint of Aztec styling. Floor-to-ceiling picture windows open out onto Oxford Street and perform two crucial functions – potential customers walking by can feel the vibe from a friendly, fun crowd and window-shop before they decide to come in, whilst customers inside check out the passing throng and, to paraphrase words sung by Andy Williams,

> 'The boys watch the boys and girls while the girls watch
> the girls and boys who watch the girls and boys go by,
> Eye to eye, they solemnly convene to make the scene.'

A huge illuminated fibreglass mask on the staircase landing atmospherically links the two main bar areas and leads from the open airy ground floor of Tarzan's domain, upstairs to the lounge where Scarface's den is decorated with warm chocolate, honey and russet tones matched with rich leather sofas, armchairs, pouffes and shag-pile carpet. These two distinctly different zones make the Colombian Hotel two venues in one – the ground floor is lighter, more casual and pubby with flat-screen television monitors showing music videos, and on the first floor, it is darker, cosier and intimate with a dance floor. Do not go in the evening expecting a quiet drink because it is regularly full to the rafters, in no small part due to the hip interiors and its location in one of Sydney's loud and lively entertainment hubs.

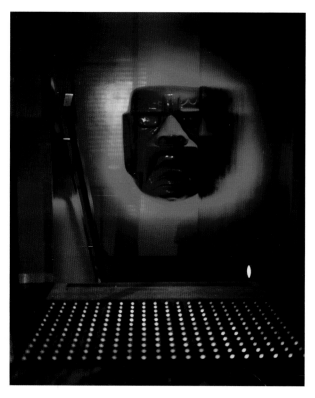

Above: The Colombian Hotel, Sydney, Australia. An illuminated fibreglass mask specially designed for the pub is situated on the landing between the two bar areas

Opposite: The Colombian Hotel, Sydney, Australia. With good people-watching opportunities through a wall of windows that open on to Oxford Street, there are few clues that this slickly designed pub was once a bank

The Colombian Hotel

Address	117-123 Oxford Street, Darlinghurst, Sydney 2010, Australia
Telephone	+61 (0)2 9360 2151
Opening hours	Daily 10am to 5am
Design style	Funky Tropical South American
Drinks	Domestic and international beers, wines, cocktails, regular pub drinks
Music	Recorded dance music
Special features	Bar snacks; licensed for dancing and live acts

Above: **The Colombian Hotel, Sydney, Australia.** Lighting levels and the rich chocolate, honey and tobacco colour scheme combine to make the lounge an intimate space

Right: **The Colombian Hotel, Sydney, Australia.** Pop art and graffiti adorn the wall of the men's loo

Left: **The Colombian Hotel, Sydney, Australia.**
Jungle graphics on the panel behind the bar, vinyl
snakeskin stools and the ethnic shape of the ironbark wood table whisper 'South America'

Right **The Colombian Hotel, Sydney, Australia.**
The cylindrical stainless-steel table in this nook
was designed by Andrew Parr at SJB Interiors

The Counting House

HC Boyes and Arc Design Associates

Location: London, UK
Completion Date: 1893, refurbished as a pub 1998

Walking through the entrance door of this pub, it becomes immediately apparent why it is called The Counting House – it looks like a bank, and was indeed a branch of the National Westminster until the 1990s when London-based brewery Fuller's bought the freehold and transformed it into one of their popular Ale & Pie Houses. First impressions are of the sharp-intake-of-breath variety because with its vast proportions, grand interior and substantial classical glass dome it is magnificent.

It works brilliantly as a pub. And being in the City of London, Britain's leading financial centre, the bank connection is a fitting historical link. The main room is large and rectangular with marble columns, dark wood wall-panelling, mint green and gilt plasterwork ceiling and mosaic floor. A superb oak and marble oval island bar in the middle looks as though it has always been there, but it was designed and constructed specially for Fuller's when the bank became a pub in 1998. On one wall a mural inspired by 18th-century artist William Hogarth (who lived opposite Fuller's Brewery in Chiswick, West London) depicts greedy moneylenders counting cash and ignoring the pleas of neighbours warning of the encroaching Great Fire of London.

Huge arched windows open up the building's facade and several super-sized gilt-framed mirrors hung high on the walls do the trick in reflecting light into the interior. An attractive staircase, installed during the refurbishment, leads to a mezzanine floor edged with a wooden rail and fancy gilt balustrades and furnished with tables and chairs. On the ground floor, high-backed leather armchairs and chesterfield sofas are arranged in a seating area with walls adorned by paintings of 18th- and 19th-century characters and despite it being a spacious pub, it has the intimate atmosphere of a gentlemen's club from another era.

Sit down with a pint of Fuller's award-winning cask ale (the brewery is a five-time winner of Beer of the Year) and one of the celebrated homemade pies – perhaps a Chicken, Ham and Tarragon, or Sweet Potato and Goat's Cheese – and try to guess what is downstairs in the private basement. Well yes, the beer cellars in subterranean bank vaults are there, but this mystery object is something much older. It is the remains of a basilica, because The Counting House is built on the site of the Roman Forum – heart of Londinium and the largest building in AD 100 Britain. Which means that when you're trying to catch the attention of the bar staff to order a drink, you are justified in saying 'Friends, Romans, countrymen, pour me your beers'.

Above: **The Counting House, London, UK.**
The oval-shaped bar island looks Victorian but was newly constructed for the pub in 1998

Opposite: **The Counting House, London, UK.**
First impressions of the grand former bank

The Counting House

Address	50 Cornhill, London EC3V 3PD, UK
Telephone	+44 (0)20 7283 7123
Opening hours	Mon-Fri 11am to 11pm
Design style	Grand Classical Victorian former bank
Drinks	Fuller's real ales, international lagers, good wine list, regular pub drinks
Music	None
Special features	Extensive menu, pub grub and homemade pies

Right: The Counting House, London, UK.
The pub serves the full range of Fuller's popular cask ales

Left: The Counting House, London, UK.
A wooden staircase leads to balcony seating

Above: The Counting House, London, UK. The foot-rail is supported by brass griffins, a reference to Fuller's Griffin Brewery at Chiswick, London

Above: The Counting House, London, UK.
A detail on the elaborate wooden bar

De Ultieme Hallucinatie

Paul Hamesse, Fred Dericks and Kris Haepers

Location: Brussels, Belgium
Completion Date: 1904 and 1981

Never was a name so fitting as *De Ultieme Hallucinatie*, because behind the understated exterior facade of an elegant townhouse in the Belgian capital, exists a time capsule of Art Nouveau styling so spectacular that one might think it a hallucination.

Until 1981, this location was a family home, originally built in 1850. In 1904, Paul Hamesse transformed the house from a neo-classical interior into the Art Nouveau fantasy it is today. When current owners Fred Dericks and Kris Haepers bought the property in 1981 they turned it into a restaurant, tavern and meetings venue. The photos in this feature concentrate on the tavern rather than the other rooms.

To reach the tavern from the street, you walk through a spacious lobby across a mosaic floor, and through a billiard room containing an ornate brass and wooden chess table, at which Garry Kasparov and Anatoly Karpov once sat. On the right is the restaurant decorated in Art Nouveau style with Charles Rennie Mackintosh Arts and Crafts influences – bespoke furniture, mirrors and ornaments designed by Paul Hamesse specifically for the house and never duplicated elsewhere. Sidle past a huge chinoiserie ceramic jardinière embellished with evil-looking dragon-like lizards and up a couple of marble steps, and welcome to the tavern.

Light and airy, it was built specifically as an informal bar and brasserie in 1981 on the site of the garden. With its high ceiling, green colour scheme and volcanic-rock wall it has a grotto-like ambience, like being outside but in. Customers sit on wooden high-backed benches that despite their appearance are surprisingly comfortable. They were designed in 1930 for the Belgian railways and are the furthest-travelled seats in any Brussels bar. Unless a customer is exceptionally tall, they will discover that the benches create intimate worlds because once seated, one cannot see the people in the adjacent booths.

On the extensive drinks menu at *De Ultieme Hallucinatie* are the brands that make Brussels such a beer-lovers' paradise, including Trappist, Hoegaarden, De Koninck, Westmalle, Orval, Chimay Bleu, Duvel and Leffe. So order a drink, sit down and think of a reason to rent the first-floor rooms – it's not often one comes across an Art Nouveau Jewish Freemasons' Lodge, but it's there above the tavern and is just one of the extraordinary features of this unique building.

Above: **De Ultieme Hallucinatie, Brussels, Belgium.** A corner of the beer garden outside the Orangerie at night

Opposite: **De Ultieme Hallucinatie, Brussels, Belgium.** The beer garden between the tavern and the Orangerie

De Ultieme Hallucinatie

Address	316 Rue Royale, 1210 Brussels, Belgium
Telephone	+32 (0)2 217 0614
Opening hours	Mon-Fri 11am to 2am Sat-Sun 5pm to 3am
Design style	Garden conservatory in Art Nouveau treasure trove
Drinks	Wide selection of Belgian and international beers, wine, regular pub drinks
Music	Recorded
Special features	Bar snacks and light meals

Opposite: **De Ultieme Hallucinatie, Brussels, Belgium.** Peering through a stained-glass window from the chess and billiard room into the garden tavern

Right: **De Ultieme Hallucinatie, Brussels, Belgium.** An Art Deco beauty adorns the wall of the tavern

Above: **De Ultieme Hallucinatie, Brussels, Belgium.** This marble goddess formerly stood in the garden pond

Left: **De Ultieme Hallucinatie, Brussels, Belgium.** An ornate staircase leads to the grand function rooms on the first floor

Left: **De Ultieme Hallucinatie, Brussels, Belgium.** The stained glass above the bar servery was originally the covered walkway through the garden between the house and the Orangery

Above: **De Ultieme Hallucinatie, Brussels, Belgium.** The entrance lobby welcomes visitors to a unique Art Nouveau restaurant and garden tavern

Right: **De Ultieme Hallucinatie, Brussels, Belgium.** The high-backed green wooden benches were designed in 1930 for use on Belgian trains

Right: De Ultieme Hallucinatie, Brussels, Belgium. Decorative stained glass above the bar

Guinness Storehouse

AH Hignett; refurbished by RKD Architects and Imagination

Location: Dublin, Ireland
Completion Date: 1904 and 2000

How to prospect for Irish black gold:

1. Hold a glass at an angle to the beer tap.
2. Pull the handle to a horizontal position.
3. Fill the glass until it is three-quarters full.
4. Allow the beer to settle completely.
5. Top the beer off by pushing the handle forward slightly.
6. Allow the head to rise just above the rim.
7. Take a sip from a perfect pint of Guinness.
8. Now visit the mother lode and compare.

Lovers of the celebrated Irish stout make the pilgrimage in droves to the Guinness Storehouse, located in what had been an abandoned fermentation plant within the main brewing complex. Now this historically significant and listed seven-storey brick building contains a modern glass and steel visitor centre where the story of the black stuff is related. On the way in, look down at the floor of the atrium where the contract signed in 1759 by Sir Arthur Guinness for the brewery site is set. The company is only a fraction into the 9,000-year lease, though the rent of 45 Irish punts per annum has most likely increased.

After learning about the brewing process and associated skills that combine to create the unique brand, take a look at the Source Bar on the fifth floor, where a serpentine structure conceals pipes that transport Guinness from the brewery to the pumps. The bar interior is industrial in style with girders, ceramic brick walls and slate floors – relating back to the construction of the original steel-framed building, influenced by the Chicago School style of architecture.

Each visitor to the Storehouse is handed a palm-sized Lucite pebble that contains a droplet of beer and entitles him or her to a complimentary tipple. To redeem it, they take an elevator to the roof and step out ('Wow! Where am I?') into the circular glass minimalist Gravity Bar with a breathtaking panorama of Dublin. Exchange the pebble for an unrivalled pint of Guinness, then grab one of the blue Arne Jacobsen 'Swan' chairs on the perimeter and thrill at this unique vantage point.

Ireland's capital has few high-rise buildings, so the view is unimpeded. If there had to be only one reason why the Guinness Storehouse is Ireland's Number 1 tourist destination, then this is it. At night when the Gravity Bar's lights are illuminated, sitting atop a 30-metre-high atrium in the shape of a giant glass that rises up the core of the Storehouse, it resembles the creamy head of a pint of Guinness. Pure genius.

Above: Guinness Storehouse, Dublin, Ireland. The Source Bar is a modern industrial design in a building notable for being the first steel-framed multi-storey structure in the British Isles when built in 1904

Opposite: Guinness Storehouse, Dublin, Ireland. For the Source Bar, local students designed a serpentine tube that conceals pipes of Guinness leading from the source to the bar

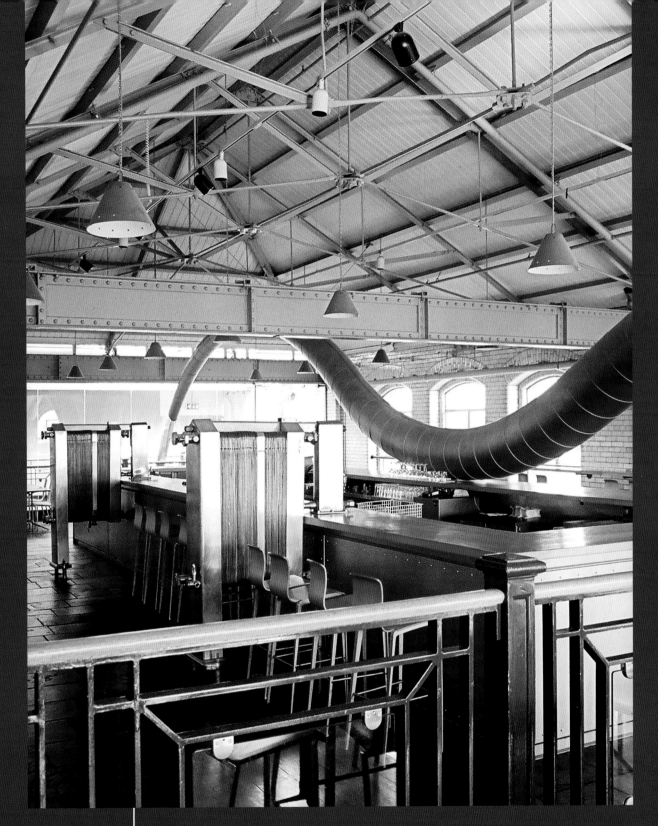

Guinness Storehouse

Address	St James's Gate, Dublin 8, Ireland
Telephone	+353 (0)1 408 4800
Opening hours	Jan-Jun and Sept-Dec – Daily 9.30am to 5pm Jul-Aug – Daily 9.30am to 8pm
Design style	Gravity Bar – Minimalist Source Bar – Industrial
Drinks	Guinness and soft drinks
Music	None
Special features	Admission charge

Above: **Guinness Storehouse, Dublin, Ireland.**
A mirror-topped table reflects the Milky Way-like
ceiling (and lighting fixtures) of the Gravity Bar

Right: **Guinness Storehouse, Dublin, Ireland.**
Unrivalled views over Dublin from the Gravity Bar

Right: **Guinness Storehouse, Dublin, Ireland.**
Visitors to the Storehouse receive a complimentary
pint of Guinness

Manor Farm Barn

Martin Godden at Shepherd Neame

Location: Southfleet, Kent, UK
Completion Date: 1747 and 2001-2

Manor Farm Barn is proof that the craftsmanship required for barn building and thatching is not dead. Take a look inside the pub at the oak frame of the barn and examine close-up the skill involved in fitting together the beams with lapped dovetails, mortice, tusk and tenon joints and timber pegs. And what a magnificent long straw thatched roof it has – such a neat job with not a reed out of place.

Kent brewer Shepherd Neame bought the structure from a farmer and transformed it to an award-winning pub in 2001–2. Originally built in 1747, it was used as a threshing barn for generations and in its latter years for grain storage. The thatched roof had been replaced in the 1930s by white asbestos sheeting – hastily painted black during World War II when enemy bombers used it as a landmark. During its construction as a pub, 65 per cent of the timber frame had to be replaced and the roof re-thatched by craftsmen who retain traditional rural skills.

But this is no twee barn conversion with cartwheels, hay bales and horse brasses. Manor Farm Barn is open, airy and light with west-facing picture windows that frame the sunset. A trellis-pattern slate floor and endless wonderful wood used for floorboards, chairs, tables, beams and the bar greet customers. The pub has a contemporary rustic look more like someone's home, with rugs, standard lamps, leather sofas and armchairs, and a wood-burning fire. Customers are encouraged to take their time and relax, read the newspapers – no pressure to vacate their seats. Designer Martin Godden likes to create rooms within rooms, each with a distinct personality, in Shepherd Neame pubs. The lounge area by the fireplace, for instance, is intimate and good for hanging out or getting to know someone in. On the first floor there is a large restaurant with a close-up view of the barn's beautiful timber frame. Typically people are reluctant to go upstairs where they feel cut off from the pub atmosphere, so this was overcome by creating a mezzanine level between the lounge and the dining room. From here, one can appreciate the modern hand-blown pink glass and fibre-optic chandelier commissioned from artist Anthony Critchlow, an eye-catching feature of the pub.

Residents and visitors of North Kent are so lucky to have Manor Farm Barn with its distinctive interior and an ambience that makes one want to stay a while. Thanks to the insulation qualities of the thatched roof, the pub is cool in summer and warm in winter – a perfect year-round climate for sampling Shepherd Neame's renowned beers. How about Whitstable Bay Organic Ale, the ideal accompaniment to a Camembert and avocado salsa sandwich from the imaginative home-made bar snacks menu, followed by a cup of Fairtrade coffee sitting by the fire that burns fragrant applewood. Flawless.

Above: **Manor Farm Barn, Southfleet, Kent, UK.** The pub sign showing how the barn might have looked in the 18th century

Opposite: **Manor Farm Barn, Southfleet, Kent, UK.** Diners in the restaurant have a great vantage point to admire the barn's superb timber frame

Manor Farm Barn

Address	New Barn Road, Southfleet, Dartford, Kent DA13 9PU, UK
Telephone	+44 (0)1474 834 967
Opening hours	Mon-Sat 11am to 11pm Sun 12 noon to 10.30pm
Design style	Contemporary rustic barn conversion
Drinks	Shepherd Neame real ales, international lagers, extensive wine list, regular pub drinks
Music	None
Special features	A la carte menu and bar snacks

Left: Manor Farm Barn, Southfleet, Kent, UK.
Roses, lavender and rosemary enhance the pretty
beer garden

Left: Manor Farm Barn, Southfleet, Kent, UK.
A selection of traditional ales from England's oldest brewer, Shepherd Neame

Above: Manor Farm Barn, Southfleet, Kent,
UK. A wall of beer lines the back of the bar

Right: Manor Farm Barn, Southfleet, Kent, UK.
The pub is situated in a former threshing barn
built in 1747

Right: **Manor Farm Barn, Southfleet, Kent, UK.**
Original beams and locally sourced replacement
oak combine in the cavernous ceiling

Above: **Manor Farm Barn, Southfleet, Kent, UK.** The pub's focal point and the most popular seats in the house

Left: **Manor Farm Barn, Southfleet, Kent, UK.** Wood, wood, glorious wood – a view of the main bar area from the front door

The Salisbury

John Cathles Hill and CYMK Architecture and Design

Location: London, UK
Completion Date: 1899 and 2003

For an atmospheric introduction to this marvellous pub, visit on a weekday afternoon when it is quiet and the spirits of former customers can be sensed. Walking through a tiled and mirrored entrance off Green Lanes over a mosaic floor towards the Saloon Bar is an especially moody entrée to The Salisbury. Heavy velvet curtains flank a proscenium arch and suggest the theatre, which is what gin palaces like this provided: an escapist fantasy for poorer people who were probably living in austere circumstances. But ironically, the very people who needed the diversion would not have entered this part of the pub – the grand sections were for gentlemen. Plebs drank in the plainly decorated public bars at the front of The Salisbury.

What had been a sumptuous pub, built in 1899 to the designs of builder-cum-architect John Cathles Hill, was one century later a faded centenarian rescued by the Remarkable Restaurants Group, specialists in restoring decaying heritage pubs. Black and white Italian marble tiles were mined from the original Roman quarries at Carrara, shipped to London and laid on the vast floor-space of The Salisbury, replacing a shabby carpet. Nowadays the pub has three bars, although with several street entrances it is likely there were originally additional separate drinking rooms patronised according to class. They are serviced by an enormous rectangular wooden bar unit backed by an elaborate gantry decorated with classical columns and mirrors, a bust of Apollo and glass cases of stuffed animals. As one might expect in a meticulously restored Victorian public house, there is a wooden screen inset with etched glass that divides two of the bars, the ceiling is embellished with

Above: **The Salisbury, London, UK.** Apollo, the patron of poets and musicians, protects performers at The Salisbury's regular music and poetry evenings

Left: **The Salisbury, London, UK.** Stuffed animals and a classical bust stand next to the TV above the bar

Opposite: **The Salisbury, London, UK.** Theatrical archways and heavy velvet curtains in the Saloon Bar

The Salisbury

Address	1 Grand Parade, Green Lanes, Harringay, London N4 1JX, UK
Telephone	+44 (0)20 8800 9617
Opening hours	Mon-Thur 5pm to 1am Fri-Sat 12 noon to 3am Sun 12 noon to 12 midnight
Design style	Theatrical Victorian
Drinks	Fuller's real ales, international lagers, wine, regular pub drinks
Music	Yes
Special features	A la carte menu and bar snacks; special events and live entertainment

Left: The Salisbury, London, UK. The Saloon Bar leads into the Dining Room, formerly used for billiards

Right: **The Salisbury, London, UK.** High ceilings make an already huge pub look even bigger

Below: **The Salisbury, London, UK.** The rectangular island bar can serve customers on all four sides

panels of cream plasterwork and decorated by stencilled thistles and flowers, and throughout the pub there is much finely carved teak panelling. It's a stunning interior, and all the more special knowing that its decline was halted by such a sympathetic restoration.

Such a huge pub with so many entry points requires specific instructions if arranging to meet people there. It's not enough to say 'See you at The Salisbury', although trying to locate a lost friend would mean a tour around the entire place, a treat for fans of Victoriana. Given that formalised social apartheid in pubs no longer exists, I would like to propose modern-day seating arrangements for this splendid boozer – feel free to ignore. Lovers and sex-kittens will be at home in the red saloon with its snugs and curtained hidey-hole; real-ale pub crawlers and sit-reading-the-newspaper-in-the-afternoon-type drinkers might care to take over the rear bar with its parquet floor and high upright stools; work outings and adult families could claim the side bar, furnished with black dimpled leather bench seating; and girls' and boys' night-out groups should head for the bright front bar, ideal for circulating and practising chat-up lines.

If the beauty of the surroundings, Fuller's cask ale and draught Czech and Belgian lagers are not enough on their own to entice a visit to The Salisbury, there is also miscellaneous entertainment – quiz nights, poetry readings, and live jazz and blues. Who could resist?

Above: **The Salisbury, London, UK.** The pub is a Victorian treasure, saved from decay by a magnificent restoration

Above: **The Salisbury, London, UK.** A wonderful place to sit and read the paper with a drink

Right: **The Salisbury, London, UK.** Antique chesterfield sofas in the Dining Room, with an original North London Manet on the wall

Right: **The Salisbury, London, UK.** The floor tiles were mined from the Carrara quarry in Italy, which has supplied marble since Roman times

JD Wetherspoon Pubs

Harrison Ince : Lime Kiln, Liverpool, 2004; West Kirk, Ayr, 2000
r3architects : The Groves Company Inn, Swindon, 2001
Inspire Design Company : Turls Green, Bradford, 2004
Tuffin Ferraby Taylor : Winter Gardens, Harrogate, 2002
Lawrence Beckingham Field : Briar Rose, Birmingham, 2000; Metropolitan Bar, London, 2000; White Swan, London, 2000

JD Wetherspoon is a British chain of pubs with a formula of value-for-money food and drink in attractive surroundings. Many properties in the company's extensive portfolio are converted buildings with a prior function – theatres, banks, car showrooms, post offices and even a funeral parlour – some of them in conservation areas or listed by English Heritage. Design is central to the Wetherspoon philosophy and this extends to the fantastic loos, often a major attraction and talking point. It is not unusual to find sofas and chairs in the ladies', much like those glamorous powder rooms in classic Hollywood films.

Quite often potential sites have been empty for years because of changes in the market and society. Once a Wetherspoon pub moves in, it can be a catalyst for increased footfall from which surrounding businesses also benefit. Turls Green, for instance, is the anchor of a new-build shopping and entertainment destination in Bradford. And sometimes a new pub helps prevent the blight that can befall a street when a large building is vacant. The Groves Company Inn in Swindon, for example, is situated in what was once a furniture store. In that case, there were no heritage features to consider and with the switch to a pub, r3architects were able to cut away and reinforce where necessary without restriction. Conversely Hamilton Hall, in the former banqueting room of the Victorian-era Great Eastern Hotel in

Left: The Groves Company Inn, Swindon, Wiltshire, UK. A vacant furniture shop in a basic box was converted into a modern bar with simple colours and finishes, including pieces of artwork – varied ceiling heights break up the different areas

Opposite: White Swan, London, UK. Architect Lawrence Beckingham Field's concept for the redesign of this former working men's club was a contemporary reinterpretation of a 1950s interior. Original features such as the mezzanine and staircase were retained

JD Wetherspoon Pubs – see captions for details

Address	see full listings on page 212
Telephone	see full listings on page 212
Opening hours	Various – depends on pub
Design style	Varied
Drinks	Guest ales, wines, regular pub drinks
Music	None
Special features	All day food; some pubs host beer festivals; several of the company's pubs are non-smoking

Left: Lime Kiln, Liverpool, UK. Floor- and counter-level lighting give the bar servery a floating appearance. Lime Kiln is a new-build structure, so pub designer Harrison Ince started with an empty shell

Below: Lime Kiln, Liverpool, UK. Designed with an industrial aesthetic using exposed brick and hard surfaces, the colour scheme softens the look – this Liverpool pub is built on the site of a former industrial building that housed the Montserrat Lime Juice Company and is near to Lime Street, originally called Lime Kiln Lane

Above: **Turls Green, Bradford, UK.** The Lloyds No. 1 Wetherspoon brand attracts a younger clientele, and a dance floor and DJ area is incorporated in the contemporary design. Cream-coloured tiling in the bar area gives a fresh, clean approach to the servery

Above: **Turls Green, Bradford, UK.** Turls Green is the anchor of a recently built shopping and entertainment destination in Bradford city centre – the piazza seating area with giant umbrellas is reminiscent of a Continental café

London, required extensive negotiation with the local authority and rail company owner before Lawrence Beckingham Field's designs were approved.

With dozens of heritage sites, JD Wetherspoon is like the National Trust for pubs – the Sir Titus Salt, Bradford, in a Victorian former swimming baths and leisure centre, and the Union Rooms, Newcastle, boasting a 4.5-metre-high stained-glass window, are just two notable sites. In such places, existing characterful decorative and structural features are retained and contemporary insertions of a bar servery, kitchen, lighting, furnishings and original artwork transform it into a pub. New-build pubs equally try to reference the site's history: Inspire, the designers of Turls Green, incorporated two bas-relief panels that depict a couple dancing to a string trio, reflecting the fact that the current pub is built on the location of Collinson's Café, famous in the 1920s for tea dances.

Choosing the pubs to feature in this spread was not easy because there are so many interesting sites in a variety of styles and locations around the country. A new breed of anorak is emerging – one keen on architecture, design and drinking who visits Wetherspoon pubs to check out the interiors, no two being the same. Just like the people who try to have a drink in every place mentioned by *The Good Beer Guide*, doing the Wetherspoon Wander may become a time-consuming hobby – with dozens of new outlets opening each year it could be a challenge without end. How fortunate.

Below: **Winter Gardens, Harrogate, UK.** A discreet facade conceals a grand interior. Winston Churchill visited the Victorian Winter Gardens in 1900 to deliver a public lecture about his experience as a prisoner during the Boer War

Above: **Winter Gardens, Harrogate, UK.** This glamorous double staircase leads down from the street entrance and originally formed part of Harrogate's Royal Baths and Winter Garden – it survived when parts of the complex were demolished in 1938

Right: **Winter Gardens, Harrogate, UK.** A major restoration and refurbishment project offers customers an inkling of how splendid the Victorian Winter Gardens must once have been

Above: **West Kirk, Ayr, Ayrshire, UK.** There is no doubt that this was once a church – original features including the roof truss, gallery, panelling and pulpit were incorporated into the pub's interior design

Right: **West Kirk, Ayr, Ayrshire, UK.** Fittings such as the bar servery were designed with an ecclesiastical flavour in keeping with extant church furniture

Below: Briar Rose, Birmingham, UK. The building's Art Deco styling influenced the monochrome look of the bar servery

Above: Briar Rose, Birmingham, UK. Fantastic loos are a hallmark of JD Wetherspoon pubs

Below: Briar Rose, Birmingham, UK. With curvaceous ceiling forms and bold patterns, this is an Art Deco Safari

Above: Metropolitan Bar, London, UK. Gold Corinthian columns and a high ceiling make this room look more like the Roman Senate than a pub – originally it was a restaurant with apartments above, and later a recruitment centre for London Underground

Left: Metropolitan Bar, London, UK. Perhaps a dramatic soundtrack, such as the Triumphal March from Aida, should play when entering this majestic interior. Decorative shields on the coffer ceiling represent the counties that the Metropolitan Railway once served

Above: Metropolitan Bar, London, UK. The architect's design concept was to combine the existing character of the historic interior with contemporary insertions, such as the bar – the Metropolitan Line of London Underground runs through Baker Street Station below

Woolwich Pier Hotel

SJB Interiors

Location: Sydney, Australia
Completion Date: 2003

If value could be placed on a view, the outlook from the Woolwich Pier Hotel over Sydney Harbour towards the bridge and city skyline would be priceless. Originally built in 1885, the hotel sits on the water's edge in the upmarket leafy suburb of Hunter's Hill. But until the refurbishment in 2003 into a sleek and chic destination, the Woolwich Pier was the kind of rough and tough dive where the wrong type of glance might get a person thrown through the windows rather than admiring the scenery from them.

Anyone who knew the place before will recognise the external facade with its balconies and fenestration. Inside, certain original features have been retained because of restrictions on structural alterations due to its status as one of Sydney's Heritage Hotels. What has changed is the ambience, the interior design transforming the Woolwich Pier from a brawling boozer into a sophisticated pub and bistro that owes more to Grace Kelly than Ned Kelly.

Central to the hotel's makeover is a courtyard shaded by mature Morton Bay fig trees and furnished with timber decking, banquettes and tables and chairs. Adjacent Asian-inspired heated cabanas containing pastel cushioned bench-seating, billowing white curtains and huge wicker lampshades offer customers the inside-but-outside experience. Leading off the beer garden is a bright and airy new bistro and bar pavilion, with picture windows, five-metre-high ceilings, an extended bar backed by an open kitchen, Blackbutt timber floors, banquettes, spacious communal tables and, of course, that incredible view. The Woolwich Pier Hotel and its award-winning chef Colin Holt were recognised nationally for Best Bistro Food in 2004, so if the fantastic beer garden and fashionable interior design do not attract new converts to the North Shore's most stylish pub, the food will.

Upstairs on the first floor is another treat for the eyes – a wrap-around balcony that offers a panorama of the land and seascape. It leads off the cavernous Harbour Lounge, a funky space decorated in tones of chocolate, turquoise and pink, with striped carpet, soft furnishings and rooms-within-rooms separated by floral screens. Colourful armchairs, sofas and leather pouffes surround a working open fireplace – just like someone's home featured in a glossy lifestyle magazine. But the focal point of the lounge is a long white marble bar counter and servery, backed by a coral-coloured wall and two ultra-glam light fittings with nude bulbs that, depending on how much has been imbibed, resemble either Sputnik or snowflakes.

Winter or summer, the Woolwich Pier Hotel is a fabulous spot from which to admire Sydney's breathtaking harbour – and with the ferry wharf only five minutes' walk away, what could be better than arriving by water?

Above: **Woolwich Pier Hotel, Sydney, Australia.** A corner detail of the Harbour Lounge fireplace

Opposite: **Woolwich Pier Hotel, Sydney, Australia.** Several of Sydney's famous Morton Bay fig trees bring shade to the courtyard

Woolwich Pier Hotel

Address	2 Gale Street, Woolwich, Sydney, NSW 2110, Australia
Telephone	+61 (0)2 9817 2204
Opening hours	Mon-Tue 11am to 11pm Wed-Sat 11am to 12 midnight Sun 11am to 10pm
Design style	Slick contemporary resort
Drinks	Beers, lagers, cocktails, extensive wine selection, regular pub drinks
Music	Recorded
Special features	A la carte menu and bar snacks

Left: **Woolwich Pier Hotel, Sydney, Australia.** A wicker lampshade designed by Stefano Gervasoni dominates a cabana

Below: **Woolwich Pier Hotel, Sydney, Australia.** Asian-inspired cabanas are arranged around the hotel courtyard

Opposite: **Woolwich Pier Hotel, Sydney, Australia.** The new bar and bistro extension to the hotel has a light, open, airy resort appeal

Above: **Woolwich Pier Hotel, Sydney, Australia.**
Original nib walls in the Harbour Lounge are heritage features and had to be retained in the refurbishment

Right: **Woolwich Pier Hotel, Sydney, Australia.**
A corner detail of the large Harbour Lounge on the hotel's first floor

THE GREEN MAN
Beer Gardens

Given the choice of being cramped in a poky, smoky spit-and-sawdust boozer or sitting outside in a beer garden on a summer evening with a warm breeze bearing the fragrance of jasmine, what would you go for?

Ask someone to imagine a beer garden in their own land and a Czech person might think of *klobása* (a traditional sausage), table football, and live bands; a Balinese may picture the sun setting over Kuta Beach and hundreds of holiday-makers watching as it goes down; whereas a Laotian's thoughts would go to one of the popular waterfront garden-bars overlooking the River Mekong in Vientiane. In Japan, drinking in beer gardens is a summer tradition and they pop up in unexpected places – department stores, for instance, as well as the more usual hotels and parks.

The Green Man

Ideally beer gardens should be verdant and picturesque, places that bring joy to the eye. So landlords who refer to the bare concrete patio next to the car park of their pub as a beer garden should be arrested by the Pleasure Police.

Beer gardens are great selling points – that's why pubs with gardens in tourist hubs are usually packed out. Take Munich, the undisputed champ of outdoor beer drinking and its famed biergartens that lure visitors from all over the globe. The city is home to 30 such gardens, including the world's largest, Königlicher Hirschgarten with seating for 8,500, and several others that can accommodate several thousand at any one time. Even with such large numbers, the logistics of servicing the huge clientele are efficiently executed. For instance, milk floats silently trundle around the tables collecting empties – hefty glass steins that weigh a kilogram – and take them to be cleaned in industrial-sized dishwashers. If this businesslike approach sounds off-putting, worry not: it is an invisible factor that does not interfere with the fantastic experience of sitting under a canopy of foliage and endlessly toasting friends with litre-capacity mugs of foaming beer.

Mature horse chestnut trees surround most Bavarian biergartens although linden trees provided shade in the early days – the trouble was, aphids munching on the leaves left a sticky residue on tables below. After chestnut trees were introduced to Germany in the 18th century, that species began to replace linden as the beer garden emblem. In spring, their white blossom is a pretty sight and by autumn, beautiful shiny conkers litter the ground. Visitors from Britain, where binge drinking is commonplace, may be flabbergasted to sit amongst so many people drinking alcohol and yet witness no obnoxious behaviour. The Munich beer gardens featured in this section are in several locations around the city and, with their traditional food, staff dressed in Bavarian national costume, laid-back atmosphere and delicious beer, are not to be missed.

As the song muses, 'How many kinds of sweet flowers grow in an English country garden?' For the answer, check out The Harrow in the village of Hadlow, because it has a delightful beer garden full of glorious trees, shrubs and plants. Most notable are the beds of lavender planted with the help of the award-winning Downderry Nursery. In addition to looking blissful, the pub garden is also practical, with a *pétanque* piste, a play area for children and a large lawn for strolling and rolling on. England's oldest brewer, Shepherd Neame, which owns The Harrow, has a collection of rural and urban pubs, many with lovely gardens, including Manor Farm Barn, Southfleet where special hybrid tea roses called Gracious Queen, grown only by Royal Warrant holders, flourish amongst herbs and shrubs. Another notable garden, completed in spring 2006, is at Shepherd Neame's New Flying Horse in Wye. Entitled 'A Soldier's Dream of Blighty', it is a re-creation, by the original designer, Julian Dowle, of the top prizewinner at Chelsea Flower Show 2005. The show garden was a nostalgic vision of an English country pub surrounded by flowers, and represents a picture of what British World War II soldiers serving overseas missed about home.

So if the perfect German *biergarten* resembles an arboretum, and an English pub garden a glorious horticultural show, what about a beer garden down under? Australia's great weather, love of the outdoors and propensity to revel are a recipe for the best beer gardens in the hemisphere. No surprise then that in a nation where the majority of settlement hugs the coastline, some of the most popular beer gardens combine sea and sand and are situated on or adjacent to the beach. Doyles Palace Hotel in Watsons Bay, for instance, is an international tourist attraction for the views of Sydney, Norfolk pines, waves lapping the shore, upturned boats on the beach and grilled seafood washed down by ice-cold beer. Visitors do not come for the chic furniture – plastic chairs and umbrellas – but for an Aussie vibe and never-ending party atmosphere.

Newport Arms Hotel, showcased in this section, incorporates Australia's largest beer garden in an idyllic situation overlooking Pittwater waterway, a short drive from Sydney city centre. Design is considered by the owners to be an important factor in branding the business and the hotel has been extensively refurbished to appeal to a broad market. It is particularly family-friendly with several play areas for children, and a huge TV screen broadcasting sporting events. The beer garden is landscaped with manicured lawns, native and exotic trees and plants; and from all directions the wonderful view is priceless.

Perhaps the appeal of beer gardens is something innate in the human spirit that makes us long to be outside – after all, *Homo sapiens* did not emerge in Africa holding keys to the house.

The Harrow

Martin Godden at **Shepherd Neame**

Location: Hadlow, Kent, UK
Completion Date: 2003

Customers make a snap judgement of what a pub will be like inside and whether to go in by looking at the exterior. In the case of The Harrow, with its white picket fence, hanging flower baskets, gabled portico and subtle sign, they may think 'village boozer that has been done up'. And if they choose to pass by, they are missing out on a really wonderful garden and a relaxed country pub.

Hadlow in the Vale of Kent was mentioned in the Domesday Book and may date back considerably further than the 11th century, as Roman coins and pottery have been discovered there. It is in a hop-growing region and a village brewery produced beer until after World War II. But there is still a connection to Kentish brewing because England's oldest brewer Shepherd Neame now owns and operates The Harrow, and their design manager was responsible for altering it from an unremarkable public house to one with a pared-down sophistication. Natural materials – stone, worn timber, slate – and paints from Farrow & Ball in muted tones with highlighter colour add up to a design that customers notice subconsciously.

An intimate environment has been achieved by a canny layout of individual areas – not always rooms with physical margins, but sometimes what Martin Godden calls 'defensible space', using distinct furniture and décor to mark it – that customers can claim as their own. This idea of dividing a large space into separate zones is also followed in the garden by using different plantings to create boundaries. And what a great pub garden! It was planted by Shepherd Neame's former farm manager, who now runs a landscaping business, and it features a playground for children, *pétanque* piste, lawn, mature trees and shrubs, wildflowers and, most notably, a halo of heavenly lavender from nearby Downderry Nursery – home of the National Plant Collection of Lavender and Rosemary. Lavender is laid in rows of various varieties that flower at different times of the year so the glorious scent can be enjoyed most days. Benches, tables and seats are dotted about the garden, sometimes hidden by foliage making little private corners.

The garden is a central feature of The Harrow: with views through several windows, access from a number of doors, and the dining conservatory leading outside, it becomes an extension of the pub. And with outdoor heaters, even in cooler weather it can be appreciated. So, thermals on if necessary, zip up tight, order a pint of Bishops Finger and claim a seat on the terrace. If the strong ale does not relax you, the aromatherapeutic properties of the lavender certainly will.

Above and opposite: **The Harrow, Hadlow, Kent, UK.** A village pub, with a white picket fence at the front and a large conservatory at the rear, overlooking a garden complete with umbrellas and garden furniture

Below: **The Harrow, Hadlow, Kent, UK.** The brand says it all about Shepherd Neame

The Harrow

Address	Maidstone Road, Hadlow, Tonbridge, Kent TN11 0HP, UK
Telephone	+44 (0)1732 850 386
Opening hours	Mon-Sat 11am to 11pm Sun 12 noon to 10.30pm
Design style	Sophisticated country pub
Drinks	Shepherd Neame cask ales, wine, regular pub drinks
Music	Discreet background
Special features	A la carte restaurant and bar snacks

Left: **The Harrow, Hadlow, Kent, UK.** Shrubs, hedges, and flower beds create distinct areas in the beer garden, each complete with tables, chairs and benches – one around the trunk of a mature tree

Right: **The Harrow, Hadlow, Kent, UK.** A large beer garden with room for a *pétanque* piste and a children's play area

Below: **The Harrow, Hadlow, Kent, UK.** The garden is a seamless extension of the pub

Above: **The Harrow, Hadlow, Kent, UK.**
Children are welcome too

Above: **The Harrow, Hadlow, Kent, UK.**
A private spot in the garden

Above: **The Harrow, Hadlow, Kent, UK.** Antique pieces are displayed throughout the pub

Opposite: **The Harrow, Hadlow, Kent, UK.** The interiors are painted with Farrow & Ball tones with occasional highlights of bright colour

Munich Beer Gardens

Designers unknown

Location: Munich, Germany
Completion Date: Various

Thank goodness for the heat wave in 1539 when the danger of fire spreading during the brewing process led to the *Bayerische Brauordnung*, a law that banned production of beer in the summer months. Previously brewed barrels of beer needed to be stored in cool places during the warm weather, so subterranean cellars (from where the word 'bierkeller' originates) along Munich's Isar River were dug. But proximity to the water table meant that the cellars were too shallow to chill the beer adequately and linden trees were planted above them so the leaves would provide shade.

Raise a stein to King Ludwig I (1786–1868) for permitting beer to be served outside the breweries because publicans, taking advantage of the shady arbours above bierkellers, established beer gardens and these soon became a Bavarian institution. With around 180,000 seats in 30 biergartens and numerous other outdoor drinking areas in Munich alone, there is no shortage of places to sit, except perhaps during Oktoberfest when the city welcomes thousands of beer pilgrims from all over the world.

Initially biergartens were forbidden to sell food so customers were permitted to eat their own, and though the ban was rescinded, there is still a tradition for people to take picnics, decorate tables with cloths and flowers, and have parties in the gardens. Now they have their own food culture with covered market stalls selling delicacies such as *Radi* (shaved radish), *Brezen* (giant doughy pretzels), *Obatzda* (aged Camembert cheese mixed with paprika), and *Steckerlfisch* (grilled fish fillet on a stick).

Munich's biergartens are situated all over the city, in public parks, town

Above: Augustinerkeller, Munich, Germany. Augustiner lager, often called the champagne of beers, has been brewed in a monastery since 1328

Left: Löwenbräukeller, Munich, Germany. A waiter and waitress in traditional Bavarian dress

Opposite: Augustinerkeller, Munich, Germany. A corner in one of Munich's largest beer gardens

Various – see captions for details

Address	See full listings on page 210
Telephone	See full listings on page 210
Opening hours	Variable, but usually daily 9am or 10am to 1am, between mid-May and mid-September
Design style	Traditional beer garden
Drinks	Local beers and soft drinks
Music	Some have oompah bands
Special features	Bavarian beer garden delicacies

Left: Paulaner Bräuhaus, Munich, Germany.
A quiet afternoon in one of Munich's more intimate beer gardens

squares, attached to beer halls and in residential areas. They may all have leafy trees in common, but each of the six locations featured here has its own personality.

Shady Augustinerkeller is huge with more than 5,200 seats and a number of individually decorated tables reserved for regulars. Its atmosphere is gently buzzing, oiled by Augustiner (the champagne of beer) tapped from wooden casks.

Tourists flock to the Chinesischer Turm in the Englischer Garten – Germany's largest public park – so busy it even has its own bus stop. Up to 7,000 people can be accommodated in a low-key beer garden with a Chinese pagoda as the focus, from where oompah bands, their members dressed in Bavarian costume, entertain the vast crowds.

Löwenbräukeller can seat 1,000 people for à la carte dining (and drinking of Löwenbräu beer from the brewery next door) or a more casual drink and nosh. Typically there are fewer tourists so it's a great place for visiting without a give-away guidebook and pretending to be a Münchener.

The L-shaped Paulaner Bräuhaus is rather an intimate beer garden, despite seating up to 1,200. It is attached to a brewpub of the same name in a residential part of the city away from the major tourist hubs.

On a warm day, finding a seat on the lakeside terrace at Seehaus im Englischer Garten may require waiting around and sending subliminal begging messages of 'drink up and move on … please' to the people sitting at the table you want. It's worth the wait, though, to watch boaters on the adjacent lake – the Kleinhesselohe See – and stare out the ducks and geese that will glide up and demand a piece of your *Brezen*.

There are great people-watching opportunities at Viktualienmarkt, a beer garden surrounded by gourmet food market stalls situated in the city centre, a minute's walk from Marienplatz. Compared with the others, it is only a small beer garden, but very popular with locals and visitors alike.

For beer drinkers, a visit to Munich is incomplete without the biergarten experience. *Prost!*

Opposite: **Chinesischer Turm, Munich, Germany.** An oompah band in traditional Bavarian costume plays regular concerts from the first floor of the pagoda

Below: **Viktualienmarkt, Munich, Germany.** A small beer garden in the city centre, round the corner from Marienplatz

Above: **Seehaus im Englischen Garten, Munich, Germany.** This beer garden on the banks of the Kleinhesselohe See, a large lake in the Englischer Garten, is a popular spot on a fine day

Right: **Augustinerkeller, Munich, Germany.** A beer garden so large that empty glasses are collected by electric milk float

Right: **Viktualienmarkt, Munich, Germany.** Squeezed in among flower, fruit, vegetable and gourmet food stalls – sit in the beer garden for a libation and scribble a shopping list

Newport Arms Hotel

Mark Bayfield, Lex Carter Architectural, Gartner Trovato Architects

Location: Sydney, Australia
Completion Date: 1880, rebuilt 1967, refurbished 1993 and 2000-5

There are a number of reasons to visit the Newport Arms Hotel, but perhaps the most striking is because it has something that no other Australian pub has – that is, the country's largest waterfront beer garden in a charming location overlooking the tranquil Pittwater waterway and Ku-ring-gai Chase National Park.

The Newport Arms Hotel has stood on this site since 1880 – at the time quite a daring location to build a hospitality business because Newport had a reputation as a haven for smugglers and bushrangers. The hotel was a catalyst that transformed the area into a respectable suburb of Sydney.

Today, with an all-embracing choice of bars, it is a democratic destination, equally attractive to a blue-collar drinker and sports fan in Newy's Bar, incorporating betting facilities; to a cocktail aficionado at the Terrace Bar; and to families in the Garden Bar and beer garden (it has several playgrounds for children). Then there is the Sunset Bar in the middle of the garden and here a quandary presents itself – what to drink as a sundowner? A glass of Australian wine from an extensive selection, or one of 18 beers dispensed by technological marvel from a single service point? Then, where to imbibe it – overlooking the water, or catching up on the cricket scores by the huge outdoor cinema screen? And choice is not restricted to what and where to have a libation. With an array of food offerings, depending on mood and wallet, customers have dozens of options. Fancy a King Island rump steak in the formal Terrace on Pittwater restaurant? Or perhaps a barbecued seafood platter at the Grill? If gourmet pizza or traditional Aussie pub grub hits the spot, then the Garden Bistro is the place.

Australians' love of the outdoors and the Newport Arms' proximity to water are represented in the hotel's design, colour, materials, and recurring sea and sailing motifs. Ship-lapped timber; corrugated tiles mimicking sandy ripples; sailcloth and canvas; curvaceous shapes and patterns that are impressionistic versions of waves; and shades of green, blue, and yellow – all combine in homage to the sea and sand.

Where possible, the hotel's designers – owner Mark Bayfield, in collaboration with Lex Carter Architectural and Gartner Trovato Architects – have 'brought the outside in' with all-weather seating, bi-fold doors, drop-down transparent blinds, and covered enclosures and walkways. The garden is an informal combination of lawns, pathways and paving, planted with native and tropical shrubs and trees including huge Canary palms. It's a beacon for local bird life. In the evening, sitting with a chilled drink looking over the waterway, waiting for the sun to set, waves lapping against moored sailboats and the fragrance of flowers perfuming the air, where could be better?

Above: **Newport Arms Hotel, Sydney, Australia.** Aussies love their beer, whether international or domestic

Opposite: **Newport Arms Hotel, Sydney, Australia.** Idyllic views of the beer garden, looking towards the Pittwater waterway

Newport Arms Hotel

Address	Beaconsfield and Kalinya Streets, Newport, Sydney, NSW 2106, Australia
Telephone	+61 (0)2 9997 4900
Opening hours	Mon-Sat 10am to 12 midnight Sun 10am to 10pm
Design style	Contemporary resort
Drinks	Extensive beer and wine menu, cocktails, regular pub drinks
Music	Recorded
Special features	A la carte menu and bar snacks; outdoor TV screen

Right: **Newport Arms Hotel, Sydney, Australia.**
The cavernous Sunset Bar leads directly into the garden

Above: **Newport Arms Hotel, Sydney, Australia.**
A sea and sand colour scheme in the Garden Bar

Left: **Newport Arms Hotel, Sydney, Australia.**
Wave-like motifs decorate the bar counter of
Newy's Bar

Above: **Newport Arms Hotel, Sydney, Australia.**
Overlooking Pittwater waterway

Right: **Newport Arms Hotel, Sydney, Australia.**
A view of the main hotel building at dusk

Right: **Newport Arms Hotel, Sydney, Australia.**
Canvas shades over the outdoor terraces resemble
boat sails

Above: **Newport Arms Hotel, Sydney, Australia.**
Cocktail time in the Terrace Bar

Left: **Newport Arms Hotel, Sydney, Australia.**
Wicker easy chairs in the Terrace Bar

JACK THE GIANT SLAYER
Brewpubs

Once upon a time, there was a group of nasty international brewing Giants that produced bland plastic beer. They dominated pubs all over the world and convinced a majority of drinkers that their brands were the ones to choose. The Giants appeared invincible. But a group of dedicated beerophiles who supped a magical fermentation with flavour, aroma, and body started to spread a message to the Giants' conquered masses that beer was supposed to have zest and taste. And lo, revolution multiplied throughout the beer-drinking universe as people began to demand microbrews. The Giants realised the game was up and surrendered. But the microbrewers were not vengeful and merely sentenced the Giants to accompany that well-known global burger chain and those ubiquitous coffee boutiques to the Prison of Individuality where they lived off home-made food and drink for the rest of their days.

Jack the Giant Slayer

If only that fairy tale were true. But hang on – elements of it are, because hundreds of brewpubs around the world produce beers of great character. Portland, Oregon, for instance, America's capital of handcrafted beers, has over 40 microbreweries and is often referred to as 'Munich on the Willamette'. Almost every week a beer festival somewhere in the world draws thirsty crowds; and the number of generic lager drinkers who are converting to real ale is increasing. So in a tiny way Jack is slaying the Giant – death through a thousand cuts.

Brewpubs are not a new trend; English monks were brewing beer at the Blue Anchor, Helston in Cornwall over 600 years ago, and don't forget all those medieval brewers who invited people into their house to buy home-brew. Perhaps brewpubs feel like a recent phenomenon because the hegemony of global brewing companies and their international labels is so entrenched that something independent with a distinctive personality seems novel. In the timescale of brewpub history, the four featured in this section are recent additions. What they have in common is a commitment to the hands-on production of beer and the undoubted theatre that the presence of mash tuns and copper kettles brings to a customer's pub experience. The current era of industrialised anonymous food and beverage production detaches us from what we eat and drink. Brewpubs restore the connection by providing customers with a chance to sup something special that has been made almost in front of their eyes.

Galbraith's Alehouse in Auckland, New Zealand is situated in a former Carnegie library. The brewery is one wing of the building, separate from the pub in the other. Galbraith's produces English-style real ales – the only brewery in New Zealand to do so – and they are non-carbonated and not chilled, which for certain antipodeans' taste buds may feel warm and flat. Of the showcased brewpubs, Galbraith's is the most traditional-looking, with wooden panelling and an ornate antique bar gantry rescued from a refurbished British boozer.

Each Gordon Biersch location in this American chain of brewery restaurants is individually designed – some in existing buildings and others at new-build developments. In these pubs the brewing equipment is highlighted behind windows, often with seating right up to the glass so customers can see into the brewery.

Mash, located near Oxford Circus just off London's busiest shopping street, is surprising for two reasons. Firstly, one would not expect beer to be brewed in the middle of a retail area; and secondly (throw away preconceptions of what a microbrewery should look like), Mash is a bright, futuristic space where the Jetsons, if they were real, would drop in for a pint. Real-ale-drinkers have in the past been stereotyped as bearded, woolly-jumper-wearing men. Mash dispels that image with its slick, up-to-the-minute attitude in design, food, and drinks offering. In addition to handcrafted beers devised in-house by a master brewer, cocktails and an extensive wine list ensure that the tastes of a fashionable clientele are satisfied. Mash champions the merits of real beer to a new audience who might not find it elsewhere.

Compared with Mash, Paulaner Bräuhaus in Munich could be from another world – certainly a different era. It feels like a medieval castle with barrel-vaulted ceilings, heavy stone pillars, stuffed animal-head trophies and wooden panelling, but is actually a post-war restoration of a pub built in the 19th century that resumed brewing in 1989, though one would never know because it looks authentic. Even before a customer enters the pub they will guess it is a brewery as the aroma (common in Bavaria's beer capital) escapes to the street. Inside, gleaming copper kettles, squeezed between Romanesque columns, dominate one corner. Here they are in the open rather than behind glass, so if a customer wants to they can reach out and touch the receptacles containing the golden nectar.

The small selection of brewpubs in this book illustrates a diversity of design. A couple of noteworthy locations not included here are Zero Degrees in Bristol and London – both minimalist – and Bunker in London's Covent Garden, an industrial space in the basement of a former warehouse.

Galbraith's Alehouse

Keith Galbraith

Location: Auckland, New Zealand
Completion Date: 1995

Many pubs claim, often erroneously, to be the oldest in their land; but without doubt, Galbraith's Alehouse has the most ancient bar top in the world. Carbon dated to 40,000 years old, the ancient wood came from one of the gargantuan Swamp Kauri trees that flourished in the forests of New Zealand thousands of years before humans arrived in the islands. Kauri trees are hardly shrinking violets and it was their immense size that made the timber so much in demand, especially in the English shipbuilding industry. The slab on top of Galbraith's bar is one single piece of wood, and measures some 10 metres by 1 metre.

Galbraith's Alehouse is a brewpub situated in what was Auckland's first branch library, funded by philanthropist Andrew Carnegie, and opened in 1912. It is fair to call Galbraith's a library of ales, with 15 brands on draught, eight of them brewed on the premises, and 60 local and international bottled beers, although the Dewey Decimal System has no place here!

At the entrance door, you can turn left for the pub or right for the brewery. Keith Galbraith learned the craft of beer-making at the Larkins Brewery in Kent, England under the tutelage of master brewer Bob Hudson, after whom one of the Galbraith's Bitters is named. The award-winning real ales Keith produces in Auckland are made from imported British hops and Scottish malt. A leading international beer critic named a Galbraith's brew as one of his Top 10 of 2000. So notable fresh beer is assured here, hand pumped directly from the cellar.

Above: **Galbraith's Alehouse, Auckland, New Zealand.** Fine craftsmanship on the gantry

Left: **Galbraith's Alehouse, Auckland, New Zealand.** The mirror and mantlepiece came from an old pub in the English Midlands

Opposite: **Galbraith's Alehouse, Auckland, New Zealand.** One wing is a pub, the other a brewery

Galbraith's Alehouse

Address	2 Mount Eden Road, Mount Eden, Auckland 1030, New Zealand
Telephone	+64 (0)9 379 3557
Opening hours	Daily 12 noon to late
Design style	A library of ales
Drinks	Galbraith's award-winning real ales, local and international beer, a wide selection of NZ wines, regular pub drinks
Music	None
Special features	Brewery on the premises; à la carte menu and bar snacks

Left: Galbraith's Alehouse, Auckland, New Zealand. Several award-winning beers are brewed on the premises

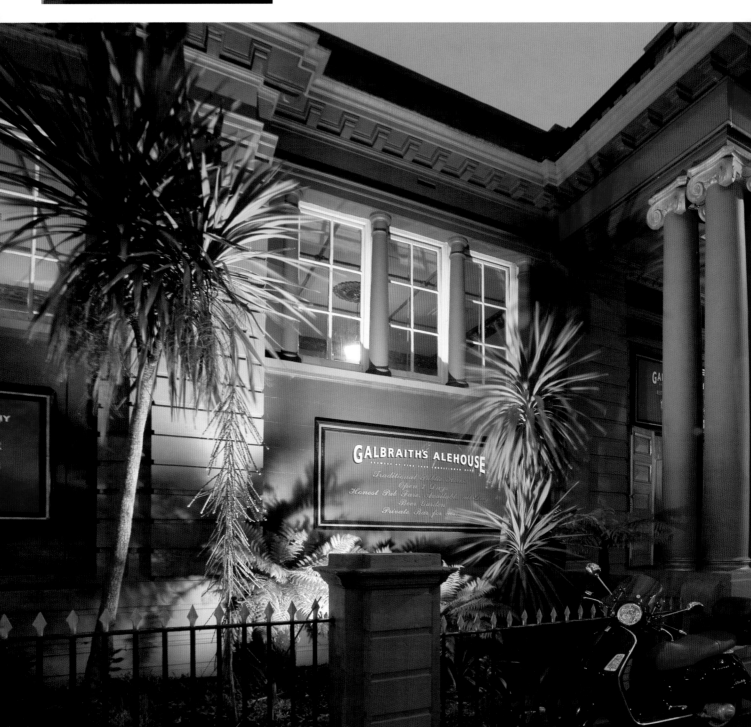

In the pub itself, the atmosphere is convivial and the surroundings egalitarian. Reminders of the library come in the wooden panelled walls that were previously lined with bookcases. Native timber is widely used, for flooring, framing, and the furniture, built from reclaimed Kauri and Rimu wood. Exposed brick coordinates with the colour of the ceiling and the overall effect of the décor is one of warmth and welcome.

Despite its recent reincarnation as a pub, Galbraith's looks as though it has been there for decades, assisted by the decorative mahogany-panelled facing of the bar counter, the ornate gantry and mirrors, and the ornamental fireplace. Inside the clock over the main bar is a repair sticker dated 1935.

You don't have to be a beer drinker to enjoy Galbraith's Alehouse; lovers of the grape should also be delighted because Keith spent 20 years in the wine industry, so his selection of over 30 wines is the choice of an expert. Whatever beverage tickles your fancy, there is a dish to go with it, be it the Neptune-worthy Coromandel Smokehouse Platter containing smoked chilli & garlic mussels served in the half shell, lime & pepper-smoked trevally, smoked peppered mackerel and smoked salmon pâté; or just plain bangers and mash.

Would it be coals to Newcastle to ask Keith Galbraith to open a branch of his library in Britain?

Opposite: **Galbraith's Alehouse, Auckland, New Zealand.** The original wooden wall panelling dates from 1912 when the pub was a Carnegie library

Left: **Galbraith's Alehouse, Auckland, New Zealand.** Corner detail of an ornate mantelpiece

Below: **Galbraith's Alehouse, Auckland, New Zealand.** The bar top is one single piece of wood from a huge Swamp Kauri tree

Gordon Biersch Brewery Restaurants

Trapp Associates : Gordon Biersch, Atlanta,1999
Architecture & Light : Gordon Biersch, Las Vegas, 1997; Gordon Biersch, Seattle, 1998
Inspire Design Company : Gordon Biersch, San Francisco, 1991; Gordon Biersch, San Jose, 1990

To undertake a definitive pub-crawl of Gordon Biersch brewery restaurants would mean having a Learjet on stand-by. With 24 locations in 13 states, that's a vast territory to cover — but worth it knowing that award-winning handcrafted beer is the prize. Gordon Biersch is the brainchild of master brewer Dan Gordon, who trained at a premier brewing school in Germany, and restaurateur Dean Biersch. Their partnership is a marriage of great beer and food brewed and prepared in good-looking surroundings.

No two sites are the same, so the architects start with a clean slate and tailor the concept to the local community. In Atlanta, for instance, Trapp Associates were mindful to create a new-build business in historic Peachtree Street that respected the heritage of the area and looked as though it had been there for decades. In the design they included classic fenestration; a loading dock to be used as a patio giving the illusion of a past history; a grain silo out front which is practical and also suggests that the site had a former use; and inside a high ceiling supported by Doric columns. The architect's efforts to ensure that the new building would not be intrusive were so successful that the Atlanta Historical Society sent congratulations believing it was an old structure that had been restored.

In terms of design and architecture, there is no corporate bible dictating a cookie-cutter approach. This means that each site has its own individuality, which also works in the architect's favour if there are problems. The Seattle branch, for instance, is based on the top floor of a shopping and entertainment destination with huge heating and air conditioning ducts that penetrated the

Above: **Gordon Biersch, San Jose, USA.** This industrial-style pub is situated in the city's downtown district — today San Jose is the heart of Silicon Valley, but it grew from a Spanish colony founded in 1777 as Alta California's first civilian settlement

Left: **Gordon Biersch, San Francisco, USA.** This pub is located on San Francisco's historic waterfront, so an industrial warehouse-style design is apposite

Opposite: **Gordon Biersch, Las Vegas, USA.** The business of brewing becomes a clean and slick work of art behind glass

Gordon Biersch Brewery Restaurants — see captions for details

Address	see full listings on page 213
Telephone	see full listings on page 213
Opening hours	Daily usually 11.30am to 11pm or midnight and later at weekends — phone for exact times
Design style	Miscellaneous
Drinks	Award-winning German-style lagers brewed on the premises, regular pub drinks
Music	Recorded

Below: Gordon Biersch, Atlanta, USA. Custom-made lighting fixtures dominate this large space and help soften the atmosphere — walnut flooring, mahogany trim, birch panelling and columns give the 'ground-up' new build structure a timeless and heritage feel

pub. To solve this ugly intrusion, Architecture & Light painted them black, and installed floating ceilings with uplights that draw the eyes away. Gordon Biersch brewery-restaurants appeal to a wide social mix and the design reflects this by being inclusive and welcoming — some sites are industrial, others sophisticated, and sometimes a combination of the two. The common denominator is the international language of beer.

Each location has an on-site brewery with equipment exposed behind glass as a feature for customers to appreciate. Year-round brews include Märzen, auburn and slightly sweet; a crisp unfiltered Hefeweizen; rich, malty Blonde Bock; and the full-bodied Dunkles. In true German style where breweries produce special seasonal and festival beers, Gordon Biersch presents Maibock to celebrate the coming of spring; Festbier, during Oktoberfest; and Winter Bock, a dark beer that was originally brewed by monks to sustain themselves during periods of fasting. Gordon Biersch specialises in brewing lagers and adheres to the stringent German Purity Law (*Reinheitsgebot*) guidelines laid down in 1516 that dictate beer must contain only malt, hops, water, yeast and nothing else. It is the commitment to brewing only German-style lagers that differentiates Gordon Biersch from the majority of US brewpubs that produce only ales.

Above: **Gordon Biersch, San Francisco, USA.** This open-plan pub situated on Embarcadero also has a patio with dramatic views of the San Francisco Bay Bridge

Left: **Gordon Biersch, Seattle, USA.** Here the design concept was to combine the slick brewing area, highlighted by purple neon, with a warehouse-style party spot — hanging lampshades above the bar resemble topsy-turvy glasses of lager

Left: **Gordon Biersch, Seattle, USA.** Concrete floors, mahogany wainscots, granite countertops and upholstery mimic the colours of the Gordon Biersch range of beer — from golden Blonde Bock and auburn Märzen through to dark Dunkles stout

Left: **Gordon Biersch, Las Vegas, USA.** A central island bar with a unit for multiple TV screens that broadcast the biggest sporting events – the bold white signage on top proclaims styles of beer brewed by Gordon Biersch

Below: **Gordon Biersch, Las Vegas, USA.** Gordon Biersch's eye-catching industrial Las Vegas branch is on a busy road leading to the airport — in a city of endless neon and visual stimuli, an attention-grabbing sign is essential to attract customers

Mash

Andy Martin Associates

Location: London, UK
Completion Date: 1998 and 2005

Once the surprise of discovering this futuristic *Lost-in-Space*-meets-*Barbarella* pub and restaurant passes, customers are in for another one – those orange and stainless-steel tanks behind the plate glass window are used for brewing beer. Without wanting to stereotype brewpubs, they do tend to be traditional or industrial in design – but funky, no. So Mash is a unique, groovy and fun addition to the pubs that carry the torch for handcrafted beer.

May I suggest that visitors choose the booth at the rear of Mash – this gives a panorama of the whole place. To the right are the lozenge-shaped wood-rimmed wall cut-outs of the bar dispensary; on the left, a sunken lounge lined with red leather banquettes and specially commissioned artwork by acclaimed artist John Currin. Remember the Coca-Cola advertisement in the 1970s where a group of healthy Americans wanted to teach the world to sing in perfect harmony? Imagine if David Lynch had been the director, it would have looked like these paintings.

Mash is a visual and sensual treat from the outset. Just inside the entrance is a florist, Absolute Flowers, with colour and fragrance to lift the spirits; then there is the Love Machine, created exclusively for the pub by Murray Partridge, styled after those devices at railway stations with black and white squares that whirl around to display a message. As a person enters Mash a sensor is activated and the machine flicks up one of a series of saucy greetings such as 'Why should I get married and make one man happy when I could stay single and make many miserable?' Throughout the pub and

Left: **Mash, London, UK.** Handcrafted beers are created in-house by a master brewer in view of pub and restaurant customers

Mash

Address	19-21 Great Portland Street, London W1W 8QB, UK
Telephone	+44 (0)20 7637 5555
Opening hours	Daily 8am to 1am
Design style	Funky Futurist
Drinks	Mash microbrewed beers, extensive wine list, champagne, cocktails
Music	Recorded and live DJs Thur-Sat
Special features	Microbrewery, pub, flower shop and restaurant all under one roof

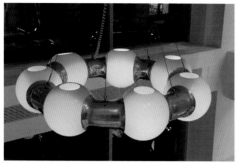

Left: **Mash, London, UK.** The atom ball-like green glass and chrome light above the main entrance

restaurant are pieces of art – a six-foot-high sculpture, a collection of stylish vases (filled with fresh flowers), and for a microbrewery, the ultimate works of art – the tun, kettle and tank that convert water, barley, hops and yeast into beer.

The beers were devised in-house by a resident master brewer and comprise four distinct brews: a fresh-tasting blond beer called Mash; Belgian Wheat with a spicy citrus tang; Festival Golden, a light fruity ale; and the amber Vienna Style Lager. For indecisive customers, a handy tasting tray of all four is offered. And to accompany the beer samples, an array of sharing dishes from an extensive menu of bar food that includes artichokes romana; Swedish-style crayfish; tomato risotto balls; and grilled lamb, coconut and coriander skewers. That's after a breakfast at Mash, of course, because it opens at 8am serving up morning treats such as portobello mushrooms on toast and mixed berry croissant with honeyed crème fraîche. Dinner is served in the first-floor restaurant. In design terms it is similar to the pub, with a glass wall overlooking the brewing equipment, but with an open kitchen instead of a bar dispensary, and with green as the dominant colour throughout. Green has great symbolism – it denotes nature, life, growth, renewal, health, balance, earthiness and warmth. In colour therapy it is soothing and relaxing physically and mentally.

Diners, who by now should be nicely Zened-out, are offered a selection of popular British dishes from a seasonally changing menu – in autumn, for instance, lamb chops with sautéed potatoes and roasted garlic; or fishcakes with sorrel mayonnaise and pea puree, followed by that all-time classic, rhubarb crumble with custard. With a late licence until 1am, that means there are only seven hours to go before Mash reopens for breakfast and the whole delicious cycle starts again.

Above: **Mash, London, UK.** The futuristic bar serves up fresh Mash brews and a smart selection of cocktails, champagne and wine

Left: **Mash, London, UK.** Lozenge-shaped runway lights on the ceiling lead the eye towards the action — orange and steel brewing tanks behind glass

Right: **Mash, London, UK.** Artist John Currin was commissioned to create the artworks for the sunken alcove

Right: **Mash, London, UK.** Red leather banquette seating and stools in the den-like sunken alcove

Paulaner Bräuhaus

Designer unknown

Location: Munich, Germany
Completion Date: 1892

If Germany had a Beer Hall of Fame, the building inhabited by Paulaner Bräuhaus would be inducted, because it was on that site in 1889 that master brewers Eugen and Ludwig Thomas presented the first Helles Münchner Vollbier (a lager beer) to the citizens of Munich. It was an instant hit and demand was so great that brewing and pub facilities had to be expanded to keep up with it. Thomasbräu was extended into the towering edifice seen today. In the 1920s, the city's brewing industry was consolidated and Thomasbräu and another local brewer Paulaner Bräuhaus amalgamated. They continued producing their popular brews until World War II when the brewery was bombed and the production of beer ceased. It limped on as a pub until an auspicious day in 1989 when Paulaner resumed brewing there.

Above: **Paulaner Bräuhaus, Munich, Germany.** An imposing building — the brewpub takes up part of the ground floor with private apartments in the storeys above

Take a look around the medieval-style interior with sturdy Romanesque columns, pointy archways, and vaulted ceilings. It's reminiscent of a 13th-century cathedral but the interiors are 20th-century restorations of a 19th-century design, though one might not guess.

Beer hounds have a highly developed sense of smell, and when walking down Kapuzinerstrasse will follow their noses to the source of the hop aroma wafting from Paulaner Bräuhaus. Walk into the pub and there on the left, niftily positioned between stone pillars, are the highly polished copper brewing kettles in which the brewery's bestselling Paulaner Hefe-Weissbier Naturtrüb, Thomas Zwickl lager, Pils, Dunkel and seasonal beers are brewed. Straight ahead are dimly lit dining rooms with heavy wood furniture and wall panels, stained glass and mounted trophy skulls of horned beasts. Bavarian specialities pack the menu, for instance *Saures Lüngerl* (stewed lung with bread dumpling), *Abgeräunter Leberkäs* (meatloaf with fried egg and potato-and-cucumber salad) and plenty of wursts. Ask for a basket of wholemeal bread – made from the brewer's grains, or 'draff', left over after the mashing process; if the beer is any indication, it's bound to be delicious. Then round off a hearty meal with a dessert of beer jelly. Yum. So that is the restaurant area; what about the remainder of the pub? On the right of the door is the beer hall, a large bright room with pillars, vaulted ceiling, and picture windows along one wall. Wooden chairs and benches accommodate customers served by waiters in traditional Bavarian costume. Tucked away behind the brewpub is a beer garden, modest by Munich standards, with seating for 1,200.

Two annual dates to mark in the diary for visits to Paulaner Bräuhaus are Lent, for the beer-blessing ceremony, and Oktoberfest when Munich invites the world to celebrate what Julius Caesar called 'a high and mighty liquor'.

Opposite: **Paulaner Bräuhaus, Munich, Germany.** Hefe-Weissbier Naturtrüb — Paulaner's number one bestselling beer

Paulaner Bräuhaus

Address	Kapuzinerplatz 5, 80337 Munich, Germany
Telephone	+49 (0)89 544 6110
Opening hours	Mon-Fri 10am to 1am Sat-Sun 9am to 11pm
Design style	Romanesque and Gothic mix
Drinks	Paulaner beers brewed on the premises
Music	None
Special features	Brewery on the premises; à la carte menu and traditional beer garden snacks

Right and far right: **Paulaner Bräuhaus, Munich, Germany.** Pipes lead directly from the copper brewery kettles, cunningly inserted between the marble columns, to the beer pump and then the glass — a fresh brew indeed

Below: **Paulaner Bräuhaus, Munich, Germany.** Marble columns support the vaulted ceiling

THE SIX YUM-YUMS
Pubs with Quality Food

London's Clerkenwell district has great revolutionary credentials: Vladimir Lenin shared an office there in 1902 during his exile from Russia, and 91 years later the Eagle pub in Farringdon Road re-opened with a new concept – to offer an imaginative menu of good food using fresh ingredients cooked by a chef in a casual pub setting. A stripped-back wooden interior of mismatched tables and chairs, comfy sofas, and clear glass windows was the look. This was the beginning of the gastro-pub revolution and it has spread widely, including to Manhattan where The Spotted Pig, run by an English chef, was the first to emulate Blighty's lead.

The Six Yum-Yums

In Britain, the gastro-pub trend is on the way out because although they were very successful in bigger cities, where people did not mind paying the prices that costly well-trained-chef-designed menus required, in other places more expensive pub food was not as warmly received. Now the demand for quality food and drink is so widespread in Britain that pubs have responded, and better-value versions of the old gastro-pub formula are proliferating. Both customer and pub are the winners, and one does not have to travel far now to find somewhere that serves great pub grub. Farewell pork scratchings and pickled eggs – but not entirely, because one rural pub I know of was recently taken over by a new landlord who could not be bothered to serve what in his part of the country are called 'bar meals', despite inheriting from the previous tenants a large clientele who travelled there specifically for the food. Instead, he kept a stash of Pot Noodles that were offered surreptitiously to regulars at 70p a time.

In Germany, Belgium, and many other European countries, it is taken for granted that food is served in pubs. In England perhaps it was the evolution of pubs from alehouses originally licensed to sell beer only that in later centuries led to hostelries where food was not considered necessary, and the lack of it became the norm. This is no longer the case, though, and some people bemoan the increasing loss of traditional boozers as they are converted into trendy pub-dining rooms.

Of the six pubs in this section, one is in Australia and the remainder are in England. In Australian cities, particularly Sydney and Melbourne, long-established pubs, or hotels as they are often called down under, are being modernised as smartly designed spaces with brasseries, bistros, and restaurants serving quality food and drinks. Australian pub owners have started to appreciate the lucrative consequences that reflecting the lifestyle aspirations of high-spending customers can bring. There is no magic formula for designing a good-food pub, as the selection in this section illustrates. In design terms they can be described as gin-palace-meets-shabby-chic; Edwardian country house; Grand Victorian; cool contemporary; and lounge-about – and if the food were not up to scratch, each pub would still attract custom on the strength of its interior.

The Black Lion in London is a splendid pub that had become a dirty, run-down spot where the beautiful interior was not appreciated. Luckily, it was rescued by a new owner who recognised its remarkable heritage. It is furnished with leather chesterfields and assorted wooden tables and chairs, none of which match – shabby chic in the shell of a former gin palace. A large space, adjacent to the main bar area, that lets in natural light was used for billiards in the 19th century when this pub was built, and it works very well as a dining room.

'Make yourself at home' springs to mind with The Catcher in the Rye, situated in a London suburb. With standard lamps, armchairs, rugs, fireplace, curtains, and a bow window, parts of it feel like being in someone's front room. This one is a real neighbourhood pub, especially popular on Sundays when a roast dinner is on the menu.

If Ralph Lauren owned a pub, it might look like the County Arms in London. It has a distinct Edwardian country house feel, homely and comfy whilst still grand. A separate dining room packs customers in and eating here feels like a special occasion.

The Formosa Dining Room is attached to a unique pub called the Prince Alfred. The restaurant is a modern and minimalist space in what were the pub's stables. It bears no resemblance at all to the remainder of the pub – which is no bad thing, particularly as it would be near impossible to match the incredible panelling, ceramic tiles, and etched and plate glass of this singular Victorian treasure.

Fine unwinding is the motto of the Salt House in Epsom, renowned for the relaxing properties of its famed salts. Like The Catcher in the Rye, this pub was designed by designLSM and has a similar feel of being a great place to lounge about in comfy sofas and chairs while waiting for a plate of great nosh.

Another faded boozer that was converted by a modern design is Sydney's White Horse Hotel, a chic location with a smart menu and stylish brasserie. Refurbishment alienated the former customers (allegedly a brawling bunch of toughies) and attracted instead a swish design-led high-spending crowd. And that is the reason pub owners are so keen to convert old pubs – it's great for business.

Black Lion

RA Lewcock and FT Callcott

Location: London, UK
Completion Date: 1898, refurbished 2003

When the Black Lion's current owner bought the pub in 2002 it was a rough, dirty boozer with slot machines, boarded windows and, most thuggish of all, sections of the elegant 19th-century woodwork painted black. What a difference two months makes – that is how long it took to restore the remarkable Victorian interior.

Thankfully many of the original features were still intact, including the fancy stucco ceiling now in gilded medallions on a burgundy background supported by Corinthian columns in matching colours; a green and gold Robert Adam-style frieze of angels, cherubs and swags that runs along each wall at ceiling height; carved wooden screens and ornate bar; and copper bas-relief panels of 18th-century figures engaged in activities such as playing bowls, or pouring ale from a jug.

Above: **Black Lion, London, UK.** The ultra-glam gold and burgundy ceiling

This is an especially attractive place in which to sit during the day, when natural light from the picture windows streams into the spacious bar area and shows off the richness of the décor. An eclectic collection of vintage chesterfield sofas and armchairs is scattered throughout the main bar, along with a variety of wooden and marble-topped tables. Nothing matches and it works beautifully in creating a comfy casual ambience perfect for lounging around in. The bar itself is a huge U-shaped island that would originally have served three rooms: the saloon, public bar, and private room – separate compartments that were screened from one another. One of these screens, resplendent with carved wood and etched mirrors, is still in place and conceals the office from the rest of the pub.

An attractive restaurant is situated in a large adjoining space originally used for playing billiards – hence the two glass skylights. Décor-wise it is an extension of the main part of the pub with the gilt frieze, and has green-painted walls hung with mirrors and modern artwork. Diners can sit either at a table or in the main bar room. There are no airs and graces in this pub restaurant.

A public house called Black Lion has stood on this site since the 17th century. The name may be a reference to the heraldic arms of Queen Philippa of Hainault, wife of Edward III; or to those of Welsh hero Owen Glendower. The present Black Lion was built during a pub boom period when gin palaces were erected in major British cities. Over a century later it survives as a member of London's most picturesque pub club.

Opposite: **Black Lion, London, UK.** A vast U-shaped wooden bar

Black Lion

Address	274 Kilburn High Road, Kilburn, London NW6 2BY, UK
Telephone	+44 (0)20 7625 1635
Opening hours	Daily 11am to 12 midnight
Design style	Grand Victorian meets Shabby Chic
Drinks	Cask ales, international lagers, extensive wine list. regular pub drinks
Music	Live music on Sundays
Special features	A la carte menu and bar snacks

Above: **Black Lion, London, UK.** A beautifully
restored Victorian treasure

Right: **Black Lion, London, UK.** A view into the pub from the street

Right: **Black Lion, London, UK.** A corner of the main bar room

Above: Black Lion, London, UK. In the restaurant, looking towards the main bar room

Left: Black Lion, London, UK. Vintage chesterfield sofas by an ornate fireplace

Right: Black Lion, London, UK. The dining room was formerly a billiard room, with two skylights in the ceiling

The Catcher in the Rye

designLSM

Location: London, UK
Completion Date: refurbished 2005

If anyone knows of another pub in Britain bearing the same moniker as The Catcher in the Rye, I'll buy them a drink. Fans of the eponymous novel might recognise the pub sign depicting an orange carousel horse, inspired by the first-edition book cover. References to the JD Salinger classic also extend to the interior, with text as artwork and clapperboard panelling inside the front door, the latter typical of New England to where the book's protagonist Holden Caulfield wanted to escape.

The Catcher in the Rye is owned by the Faucet Inn Pub Company, which specialises in transforming nondescript local boozers into stylish public houses. As well as gastro-pubs such as this one, they also own lounge dining rooms and style-bars. The company commissioned designLSM to create a modern gastro-pub that retained all the traditional values of a pub but with a contemporary twist. So the original brick and wooden interior was cleaned and exposed, and comfy seating installed. There is no doubt that this is a pub, but with the leather chesterfields some might even be reminded of a gentlemen's club. Eclectic artwork ranges from funky to ethnic to literary to pop-culture. All the furniture, fittings and decorations are new but have an eye to the past. A rich colour scheme of chocolate, tans, creams and deep grey bestows a classy polish.

It's a great place in which to play hide-and-seek, with several nooks and crannies on different levels. These six separate areas give the impression that the pub is much bigger than it is, but they also form semi-private areas, each decorated in an individual style, towards which people gravitate according to their mood or company.

If it's summer, grab that corner with the huge poppy mural covering the wall and order some food from the seasonally changing menu. How about salmon with lemon and thyme mash and lime *beurre blanc*, or Thai spiced swordfish? But during winter the sofas by the open fire will be cosier and a proper Sunday lunch is essential. And to drink, there is a well-chosen wine list, but if beer is your tipple, three guest cask ales are always in-house, along with the regular Young's Bitter and Waggle Dance, and international lagers.

There is a distinctly domestic feel about The Catcher in the Rye's niches, whether it is the leather armchairs by the bay window, the curtains, or the standard lamps. Everything about the design of this pub creates an ambience where one feels comfortable and wants to linger.

Opposite: The Catcher in the Rye, London, UK.
The pub has several distinct nooks and crannies, each with an individual look

Below: The Catcher in the Rye, London, UK.
The pub sign was inspired by the original book cover of the eponymous novel

The Catcher in the Rye

Address	315-319 Regent's Park Road, Finchley, London N3 1DP, UK
Telephone	+44 (0)20 8343 4369
Opening hours	Mon-Thur 11.30am to 12 midnight Fri-Sat 11.30am to 1am Sun 12 noon to 11.30pm
Design style	Make-yourself-at-home modern Comfy Domestic
Drinks	Guest cask ales, international lagers, extensive wine list, regular pub drinks
Music	None
Special features	A la carte menu and bar snacks

Above: **The Catcher in the Rye, London, UK.**
Rich colours and materials create a warm and
intimate atmosphere

Left: **The Catcher in the Rye, London, UK.**
Hardwood flooring and reclaimed bricks are used
throughout the pub

Above: **The Catcher in the Rye, London, UK.**
The décor. comfy furniture and bay window
suggest a private rather than a public house

Left: **The Catcher in the Rye, London, UK.**
Slick pumps dispense international brands

Left: **The Catcher in the Rye, London, UK.**
A selection of cask ales is always available

Left: The Catcher in the Rye, London, UK.
The clapperboard panelling imbues a sense of New England – to where the eponymous book's protagonist Holden Caulfield wanted to flee

Opposite: The Catcher in the Rye, London, UK.
Wrought-iron wall-hanging — one of an eclectic selection of decorative artworks throughout the pub

Below: The Catcher in the Rye, London, UK.
Furniture and fittings are all new but chosen to recall a previous era

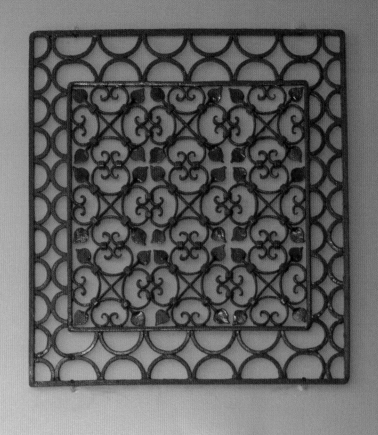

The County Arms

Neil Bardrick Associates and Young's Brewery

Location: London, UK
Completion Date: 1852 and 1890, refurbished 2003

From the inside, this elegant pub has the feel of an Edwardian country house despite nowadays being situated in a built-up suburb and on a major highway into London. However, when it was constructed the road was used by horse and carriage because the internal combustion engine had yet to be invented, and the adjacent Wandsworth Common supplied a little of the countryside in the city. During the 18th century, wealthy businessmen who had built splendid houses on the Common tried to enclose it, but they were stymied by people power, and it was saved for use by the general public. It is still an affluent corner of London with a state facility a few hundred yards from the County Arms that sits on valuable real estate indeed. Her Majesty's Prison Wandsworth was built a year before the County Arms first opened for business; this proximity is acknowledged in the pub's gents' lavatory by a 'rogues' gallery' of infamous inmates.

The County Arms received a design makeover in 2003 with the intention of creating a modern, stylish pub that was not trendy. It is comfortably luxurious with leather and upholstered easy chairs, sofas and pouffes; seagrass carpeting; walls and ceiling painted in Farrow & Ball tones; palm plants; and original artwork. Candles in medieval-style chandeliers hang from the ceiling and are placed on tables and other surfaces to give an atmospheric glow after dark. A number of original features were retained, including Corinthian columns (painted a chic gold), an ornately carved screen, stained glass, a decorative marble fireplace that is the feature of the dining room, and parquet flooring that required partial restoration.

A clever aspect of the pub's layout is the feeling of 'rooms within rooms' – defensible areas made semi-private by the positioning of comfy seating, or nooks set back from the main space. It has an atmosphere very conducive to relaxing and chatting in, or listening to live music – jazz on Mondays and blues on Tuesdays.

As befits a gastro-pub of such elegance, the menu is smart too. It features classic English favourites such as bangers and mash and more exotic fare – grilled salmon on an oriental noodle broth, with ginger shallots, lemon grass, coriander, and chilli. New and Old World wines are presented in a list for all palates, and as the pub is owned by local Wandsworth brewery Young's, the beer selection features their superstar brands of cask and bottled ales.

With an attractive all-weather beer garden, the temptation is to sit outside, but that would mean missing out on the wonderful interior. So maybe the thing to do is to have the County Arms as a pub for all seasons – go in spring and summer to sit out and salute the sky, then in autumn and winter cocoon all cosy by one of the open fireplaces and admire the fine surroundings.

Above: The County Arms, London, UK.
A mosaic at the entrance proclaims the name of the pub which has a Mock Tudor exterior

Opposite: The County Arms, London, UK. The refurbishment succeeded in creating a pub that is at the same time modern-looking and traditional

The County Arms

Address	345 Trinity Road, Wandsworth, London SW18 3SH, UK
Telephone	+44 (0)20 8874 8532
Opening hours	Daily 11am to 12 midnight
Design style	Edwardian Country House
Drinks	Young's real ales, international lagers, extensive wine list, regular pub drinks
Music	Recorded and special events
Special features	A la carte menu and bar snacks; regular live jazz and blues

Left: **The County Arms, London, UK.** A medieval-looking chandelier

Opposite: **The County Arms, London, UK.** A popular place to sit in winter when a real fire burns in the grate

Above: **The County Arms, London, UK.** A wide view of the public bar

Right: **The County Arms, London, UK.** The pub stocks both international beer brands and Young's award-winning cask ales

Prince Alfred & Formosa
Dining Room

Designer unknown

Location: London, UK
Completion Date: c. 1856, refitted c. 1898, refurbished 2001

The dictionary definition of the word 'unique' is: 'of which there is only one, unmatched, unequalled'. That certainly applies to the Prince Alfred. What makes it singular is the layout, which is exceedingly difficult to illustrate in photographs due to placement of columns, screens and the bar counter, but amazing to experience first-hand. The Prince Alfred is a survivor, with the structure of its interior little changed since being refitted c. 1898. Five individual rooms radiate off the central bar – a horseshoe-shaped island – and are separated from each other by elaborately carved mahogany screens inlaid with etched glass panels. These rooms all have their own street entrance, not always open, so access is through thigh-high door openings in the screens, originally used by the staff. Being forced to crouch down to enter a snug causes a great deal of mirth amongst the clientele, especially when tipsy. One of the snugs, the smallest, was reserved for ladies, and it retains pivoting snob screens (a feature of Victorian pubs) that can be opened for bar service and closed for privacy. According to Geoff Brandwood, author of the book *Licensed to Sell*, these screens are rare indeed, one of only two sets believed still to exist in their original location.

Not only is the interior something to marvel at, but the facade is stunning too. A flamboyant presentation of curvaceous etched glass picture windows, alternately bowed and concave, ripple around the exterior. Colourful ceramic wall tiles and a mosaic floor lead customers through the main entrance. It still dazzles today, so imagine how passers-by felt when it was built.

This expanse of windows makes the Prince Alfred an unusually light Victorian public house, all the better to admire the superb craftsmanship. Today's drinkers sit on squashy leather sofas, chairs and pouffes that convey a casual and laid-back atmosphere in a museum-quality interior. In 2001 the pub was refurbished when a space at the rear that originally housed the stables but had latterly been used as a games room was transformed into a modern restaurant. The design is understated, with a skylight roof, mint-green walls, mirrors running along the rear wall, original artwork, and a splendid Art Nouveau fireplace and mantelpiece. An imaginative menu and friendly staff have led to plaudits and recognition as one of London's leading gastro-pubs. As befits a pub with great grub, the wine list is full of delicious choices, and crisp Belgian and Bavarian lagers that go so well with food are on-tap.

Prince Alfred, Duke of Edinburgh, was Queen Victoria's second son. Alfie, as he was known, could claim a unique double: he is the only person to have had both a pub *and* the administrative centre of the British Overseas Territory of Tristan da Cunha – Edinburgh of the Seven Seas, population c. 300 – named in his honour.

Above: **Prince Alfred & Formosa Dining Room, London, UK.** Each bar room has a separate entrance — the door on the left leads into a snug that originally would have been for ladies only

Opposite: **Prince Alfred & Formosa Dining Room, London, UK.** A peek into the smallest snug, originally for ladies only — pivoting snob screens above the bar counter can be opened for service and closed for privacy

Prince Alfred & Formosa Dining Room

Address	5a Formosa Street, Maida Vale, London W9 1EE, UK
Telephone	+44 (0)20 7286 3287
Opening hours	Mon-Sat 11am to 11pm Sun 12 noon to 10.30pm
Design style	Classic Victorian pub with superb wood and glass craftsmanship
Drinks	International beer and lager, extensive wine list, regular pub drinks
Music	Recorded
Special features	A la carte menu and bar snacks

Left: Prince Alfred & Formosa Dining Room, London, UK. The extraordinary curvaceous facade would have sent a message to Victorian punters — 'If it looks like this on the outside, what must it be like inside'

Above: **Prince Alfred & Formosa Dining Room,
London, UK.** Victorian ceramic tiles run along the
wall from the street right inside the pub

Left: **Prince Alfred & Formosa Dining Room,
London, UK.** A glass ceiling filters natural light
into the dining room

Above: **Prince Alfred & Formosa Dining Room, London, UK.** A horseshoe-shaped servery services each of the bars

Left: **Prince Alfred & Formosa Dining Room, London, UK.** An aerial view of two of the bars, separated by a magnificent mahogany and etched glass screen

Right: **Prince Alfred & Formosa Dining Room, London, UK.** The mahogany gantry has an identical twin on the other side of the servery

Below: **Prince Alfred & Formosa Dining Room, London, UK.** Looking into the main bar from the restaurant — the pub's entire frontage is etched glass and carved mahogany

Salt House

designLSM

Location: Epsom, Surrey, UK
Completion Date: 2005

When Henry Wicker noticed in 1618 that cattle would not drink from a water hole on Epsom Common, the water was tested and found to contain a combination of minerals that became known as Epsomite, or more commonly Epsom salts. Ever since, the salts have been used in medicinal baths and are especially renowned for their unwinding properties. The pub equivalent of taking an Epsomite soak is a visit to Salt House – bound to heal any aches and pains caused by a busy day at work.

Before Salt House opened in its stylish and welcoming new guise, it was a run-down boozer called the Old Bank where the clientele made those in filmdom's 'Slaughtered Lamb' public house look like the friendliest in town. Originally the building was a Victorian bank and the walk-in safe with its heavy reinforced door is still *in situ* at the rear of the pub. The 19th-century provenance is reflected in the furnishings – mahogany tabletops, parquet floor, leather chesterfield sofas, flock wallpaper, and gilt mirrors. A rich colour scheme of dark chocolate, burgundy and deep red gives the pub a luxurious appearance, though still traditional, warm, and inclusive.

Salt House is operated by the Faucet Inn Pub Co, and like their other properties – including The Catcher in the Rye, also featured in this book – follows the successful formula of being a great-looking pub that serves excellent food and drink. designLSM was responsible for the 'look', and the salt-themed artwork, fresh flowers, smart food and drink selection, chic interiors and relaxed attitude are a winner with locals – whether shoppers, office workers, business people during the day, or couples and groups at night. Its layout is one open ground-floor space with four distinct areas and moods – formal seating for eating, informal tables for drinking, a bar for standing chatting, and outside a heated beer garden enclosed by high bamboo fencing.

So what is on the menu? How about this – poached salmon pitta pizza to start, beetroot and vodka risotto as an entrée, rounded off with summer fruits in champagne jelly. And to drink, a crisp False Bay Sauvignon from South Africa might complement the meal. Whilst at it, let slip a fiendishly complete knowledge of superstitions related to salt. Here are a couple – a person who spills salt should throw a pinch over their left shoulder. Explanation: in the Middle Ages, salt was so expensive that spillage was thought to bring about misfortune – evil spirits were believed to lurk behind a person's left side so throwing salt in their eyes would stop them bringing bad luck. And related to this is the tradition of sprinkling salt on the steps when moving into a new house to bring good luck. But try to avoid knocking over the saltshaker – it denotes that a friendship is about to be broken.

Opposite: Salt House, Epsom, Surrey, UK.
Behind the Classical former bank facade is a stylish pub that, as the sign suggests, is a place for fine unwinding

Salt House

Address	41-43 High Street, Epsom, Surrey KT19 8DD, UK
Telephone	+44 (0)1372 740 717
Opening hours	Mon-Thur 11am to 11pm Fri-Sat 11am to 2am Sun 11am to 11pm
Design style	Stylish Modern-traditional Lounging
Drinks	Domestic and international beer, guest real ales, good selection of wine, fresh fruit cocktails, regular pub drinks
Music	Recorded lounge music
Special features	A la carte menu, bar snacks and tapas; attractive beer garden

Above: **Salt House, Epsom, Surrey, UK.** The pub's colour scheme co-ordinates with the tones in authentic stained glass

Above: Salt House, Epsom, Surrey, UK. A cluster of oversize lampshades is a design feature placed to create interest and break up the huge ceiling of the former banking hall

Left: Salt House, Epsom, Surrey, UK. The original brickwork was restored and improved in the refurbishment

Above: **Salt House, Epsom, Surrey, UK.** The building's roots as a Victorian bank are recognised in the furniture – gilt mirrors, mahogany tabletops and leather chesterfield sofas throughout the pub

Right: **Salt House, Epsom, Surrey, UK.** Luxurious chesterfield sofas by a painted canvas of salt flats and shelf sculptures of saltshakers – references to Epsom's famous salts

The White Horse Hotel

Ron McCulloch

Location: Sydney, Australia
Completion Date: 1930s, refurbished 2004

A white horse has great symbolism – in some cultures it denotes the sun, moon, sea, the heavens, justice, and holiness; in Japan it represents divine authority; and in the Bible, Zachariah 6 : 1–7 the white horse signifies joy and victory, which would make this stylish Surry Hills pub the ideal place to celebrate placing a $50 bet on a 100–1 outsider that romped home in the Melbourne Cup.

Formerly a rough-and-ready boozer in a working-class, some might say slum, district of Sydney, the White Horse was a local to crooks, the police and, it is said, working girls touting for trade. Entertainment included a piano played by a transvestite. When the revamped White Horse first opened as a chic bar and brasserie in 2004, a customer sat in the same seat each lunchtime. Turns out it was the pianist from the old days who said that was the very spot she had played the piano for all those years.

Now a new clientele has moved in and Surry Hills is a fashionable district of cool cafés, bars, and restaurants, the White Horse being one of them. To locate it, keep looking up along Crown Street until the galvanised-steel rampant horse sculpture on top of the roof comes into view. It was made in Scotland by sculptor Andy Scott, cut into pieces, shipped to Australia, and then reconstructed on the roof. The pub's designer Ron McCulloch had a difficult time trying to persuade the local council that it was art and not advertising.

Ron describes his design as 'cool contemporary', and it is certainly slick, with its muted palette of chocolate, cream, and gunmetal grey, and use of exposed brick, soapstone and slate for floors, walls and trims. Squashy seats and sofas demand to be lounged in, the ones in the main bar offering a great vantage point for people-watching, whilst in the Upper Bar, a cosy love booth is the perfect setting for watching one of the regularly screened classic movies. Artwork is displayed throughout the pub – a buddha and abstract sculptures in the Suite; a sculpted male torso showing off its six-pack abs on the Terrace – and vases full of gorgeous flowers in all rooms add splashes of colour.

Such stylish surroundings deserve food of a fittingly high standard. The changing menu is a smart offering of ingredients that reflects Australia's ethnic mix: for instance, bruschetta of Persian feta, zucchini, mint, lemon and rocket; or seared Japanese scallops, kipfler potatoes, aioli and crispy leeks; matched with whichever style of Aussie wine or boutique beer takes the fancy.

And what about the ambience? Fabulous and friendly with a casual pub atmosphere.

Above: **The White Horse Hotel, Sydney, Australia.** The White Horse showing off its etchings

Opposite: **The White Horse Hotel, Sydney, Australia.** The pub's 1930s facade was restored to pure white

The White Horse Hotel

Address	381-385 Crown Street, Surry Hills, Sydney, NSW 2010, Australia
Telephone	+61 (0)2 8333 9999
Opening hours	Mon-Sat 12 noon to 1am Sun 12 noon to 10.30pm
Design style	Cool contemporary
Drinks	Domestic and international beers, extensive wine list, cocktails, regular pub drinks
Music	Recorded
Special features	A la carte menu in the Brasserie

Opposite: **The White Horse Hotel, Sydney, Australia.** A love booth in the Upper Bar

Above: **The White Horse Hotel, Sydney, Australia.** Canny positioning of a huge mirror makes the Terrace seem bigger and gives customers somewhere to check out how gorgeous they look

Left: **The White Horse Hotel, Sydney, Australia.** Quilted maplewood shelving and *objets d'art* surround the screen in the Suite

Left: **The White Horse Hotel, Sydney, Australia.** Classic movies are screened in the Upper Bar

Left: **The White Horse Hotel, Sydney, Australia.**
Slate panels surrounding the bar complement
the stainless-steel fixtures to suggest an overall
metallic effect

Left: **The White Horse Hotel, Sydney, Australia.**
An elegant streamlined door handle hints at the
1930s era when the White Horse was built

Right: **The White Horse Hotel, Sydney,
Australia.** The Main Bar and Brasserie with slick
stone and marble servery area in the background

Right: **The White Horse Hotel, Sydney, Australia.** The galvanised-steel stallion by Scottish sculptor Andy Scott

Beer – A Truly International Brew

Forget English or Esperanto, the real global language is beer. In all but a handful of the world's countries, beer is brewed or drunk. Even in remote Timbuktu, a visit to a millet beer bar is mandatory, and North Korea may not be able to feed its citizens adequately, but it manages to brew Taedonggang beer. Some rather unexpected nations export beer – Laos and its Beerlao; Bumthang Beer from Bhutan, and the Mongolian Baadog brew are just three.

The Pitfield Beer Shop stocks more than 600 international and domestic brands of beer, and the adjacent Pitfield Brewery produces award-winning organic cask and bottled brews such as Black Eagle, Shoreditch Stout and Eco Warrior. For customers who cannot shop in person, the mail order service is an excellent alternative.

A minuscule selection of Pitfield Beer Shop merchandise is featured in the photographs.

The Beer Shop & Pitfield Brewery
14 Pitfield Street
London N1 6EY
UK
tel: +44 (0)20 7739 3701
www.pitfieldbeershop.co.uk

Australia
Coopers Vintage Ale

Belgium
Bellevue Framboise Lambic

Canada
Sleeman Honey Brown Lager

France
St Omer Blonde Bière

Germany
Hacker-Pschorr Naturtrübes Kellerbier

Ireland
O'Hara's Celtic Stout

New Zealand
Speight's Pride of the South Gold Medal Ale

Poland
Okocim Pilsner

Russia
Baltika Lager

Scotland
Old Jock Ale

China

Tsingtao Lager

Czech Republic

Velkopopovicky Kozel
Premium Golden Lager

England

Pitfield Brewery Eco
Warrior Premium Pale Ale

Estonia

Le Coq Lager

Italy

Peroni Gran Riserva Birra
Doppio Malto

Lithuania

Svyturys Ekstra

Mexico

Negra Modelo

Spain

Cruzcampo Pilsen Beer

Sri Lanka

Lion Dark Beer

Trinidad

Carib Lager

Ukraine

Obolon Lager

USA

Liberty Ale

The Pubs – UK

United Kingdom

The Bell
The Green
Tanworth-in-Arden
Solihull
West Midlands B94 5AL
tel: +44 (0)1564 742 212
www.thebellattanworthinarden.co.uk

Black Friar
174 Queen Victoria Street
Blackfriars
London EC4V 4EG
tel: +44 (0)20 7236 5474

Black Lion
274 Kilburn High Road
Kilburn
London NW6 2BY
tel: +44 (0)20 7625 1635
www.blacklionguesthouse.com

Briar Rose
25 Bennetts Hill
Birmingham B2 5RE
Tel: +44 (0)121 634 8100
www.jdwetherspoon.co.uk

Café Royal
17–19 West Register Street
Edinburgh EH2 2AA
tel: +44 (0)131 556 4124

The Catcher in the Rye
315–319 Regent's Park Road
Finchley
London N3 1DP
tel: +44 (0)20 8343 4369
www.faucetinn.com

The Counting House
50 Cornhill
London EC3V 3PD
tel: +44 (0)20 7283 7123

The County Arms
345 Trinity Road
Wandsworth
London SW18 3SH
tel: +44 (0)20 8874 8532
www.countyarms.co.uk

Crown Liquor Saloon
46 Great Victoria Street
Belfast BT2 7BA
Northern Ireland
tel: +44 (0)28 9027 9901
www.crownbar.com

Drift
1-6 Salisbury Building
Alcester Road
Moseley
Birmingham B13 8JE
tel: +44 (0)121 449 3340

The George Inn
George Inn Yard
77 Borough High Street
Southwark
London SE1 1NH
tel: +44 (0)20 7407 2056

The Groves Company Inn
22–23 Fleet Street
Swindon
Wiltshire SN1 1RQ
tel: +44 (0)1793 402 040
www.jdwetherspoon.co.uk

The Guildford Arms
1 West Register Street
Edinburgh EH2 2AA
tel: +44 (0)131 556 4312
www.guildfordarms.com

The Harrow
Maidstone Road
Hadlow
Tonbridge
Kent TN11 0HP
tel: +44 (0)1732 850 386
www.shepherd-neame.co.uk

Lime Kiln
Fleet Street/Concert Square
Liverpool L1 4NR
tel: +44 (0)151 702 6810
www.jdwetherspoon.co.uk

Manor Farm Barn
New Barn Road
Southfleet
Dartford
Kent DA13 9PU
tel: +44 (0)1474 834 967
www.shepherd-neame.co.uk

Mash
19–21 Great Portland Street
London W1W 8QB
tel: +44 (0)20 7637 5555
www.mashbarandrestaurant.com

Metropolitan Bar
7 Station Approach
Marylebone Road
London NW1 5LA
tel: +44 (0)20 7486 3489
www.jdwetherspoon.co.uk

The New Flying Horse
Upper Bridge Street
Wye
Ashford
Kent TN25 5AN
tel: +44 (0)1233 812297
www.shepherd-neame.co.uk

The Philharmonic
  Dining Rooms
36 Hope Street
Liverpool L1 9BX
tel: +44 (0)151 707 2837

Prince Alfred &
  Formosa Dining Room
5a Formosa Street
Maida Vale
London W9 1EE
tel: +44 (0)20 7286 3287

The Salisbury
1 Grand Parade
Green Lanes
Harringay
London N4 1JX
tel: +44 (0)20 8800 9617

Salt House
41–43 High Street
Epsom
Surrey KT19 8DD
tel: +44 (0)1372 740 717
www.faucetinn.com

Sun Inn
7 Church Road
Barnes
London SW13 9HE
tel: +44 (0)20 8876 5256

Turls Green
Unit D, Centenary Square
Bradford BD1 1HY
tel: +44 (0)1274 718 330
www.jdwetherspoon.co.uk

The Vines
81–89 Lime Street
Liverpool L1 1JQ
tel: +44 (0)151 709 3977

Warrington Hotel
93 Warrington Crescent
Maida Vale
London W9 1EH
tel: +44 (0)20 7286 2929

West Kirk
58a Sandgate
Ayr
Ayrshire KA7 1BX
tel: +44 (0)1292 880 416
www.jdwetherspoon.co.uk

White Swan
255–256 Upper Street
Islington
London N1 1RY
tel: +44 (0)20 7288 9050
www.jdwetherspoon.co.uk

Winter Gardens
Unit 4, Royal Baths
Harrogate HG1 2RR
tel: +44 (0)1423 877 010

The Harrow
Maidstone Road
Hadlow
Tonbridge
Kent TN11 0HP
tel: +44 (0)1732 850 386
www.shepherd-neame.co.uk

Lime Kiln
Fleet Street/Concert Square
Liverpool L1 4NR
tel: +44 (0)151 702 6810
www.jdwetherspoon.co.uk

Manor Farm Barn
New Barn Road
Southfleet
Dartford
Kent DA13 9PU
tel: +44 (0)1474 834 967
www.shepherd-neame.co.uk

Mash
19–21 Great Portland Street
London W1W 8QB
tel: +44 (0)20 7637 5555
www.mashbarandrestaurant.com

Metropolitan Bar
7 Station Approach
Marylebone Road
London NW1 5LA
tel: +44 (0)20 7486 3489
www.jdwetherspoon.co.uk

The New Flying Horse
Upper Bridge Street
Wye
Ashford
Kent TN25 5AN
tel: +44 (0)1233 812297
www.shepherd-neame.co.uk

The Philharmonic
   Dining Rooms
36 Hope Street
Liverpool L1 9BX
tel: +44 (0)151 707 2837

Prince Alfred &
   Formosa Dining Room
5a Formosa Street
Maida Vale
London W9 1EE
tel: +44 (0)20 7286 3287

The Salisbury
1 Grand Parade
Green Lanes
Harringay
London N4 1JX
tel: +44 (0)20 8800 9617

Salt House
41–43 High Street
Epsom
Surrey KT19 8DD
tel: +44 (0)1372 740 717
www.faucetinn.com

Sun Inn
7 Church Road
Barnes
London SW13 9HE
tel: +44 (0)20 8876 5256

Turls Green
Unit D, Centenary Square
Bradford BD1 1HY
tel: +44 (0)1274 718 330
www.jdwetherspoon.co.uk

The Vines
81–89 Lime Street
Liverpool L1 1JQ
tel: +44 (0)151 709 3977

Warrington Hotel
93 Warrington Crescent
Maida Vale
London W9 1EH
tel: +44 (0)20 7286 2929

West Kirk
58a Sandgate
Ayr
Ayrshire KA7 1BX
tel: +44 (0)1292 880 416
www.jdwetherspoon.co.uk

White Swan
255–256 Upper Street
Islington
London N1 1RY
tel: +44 (0)20 7288 9050
www.jdwetherspoon.co.uk

Winter Gardens
Unit 4, Royal Baths
Harrogate HG1 2RR
tel: +44 (0)1423 877 010
www.jdwetherspoon.co.uk

The Pubs – rest of the world

Australia

The Colombian Hotel
117–123 Oxford Street
Darlinghurst
Sydney
NSW 2010
tel: +61 (0)2 9360 2151

Cruise Bar
Overseas Passenger Terminal
West Circular Quay
Sydney
NSW 2000
tel: +61 (0)2 9251 1188
www.cruisebar.com.au

Newport Arms Hotel
Beaconsfield & Kalinya Streets
Newport
Sydney
NSW 2106
tel: +61 (0)2 9997 4900
www.newportarms.com.au

The White Horse Hotel
381–385 Crown Street
Surry Hills
Sydney
NSW 2010
tel: +61 (0)2 8333 9999
www.thewhitehorse.com.au

Woolwich Pier Hotel
2 Gale Street
Woolwich
Sydney
NSW 2110
tel: +61 (0)2 9817 2204
www.woolwichpierhotel.com.au

Belgium

A la Mort Subite
7 rue Montagne-aux-Herbes-
  Potagères
1000 Brussels
tel: +32 (0)2 513 1318
www.alamortsubite.com

L'Archiduc
6 rue Antoine Dansaert
1000 Brussels
tel: +32 (0)2 512 0652
www.archiduc.net

De Ultieme Hallucinatie
316 Rue Royale
1210 Brussels
tel: +32 (0)2 217 0614
www.ultiemehallucinatie.be

Falstaff
19 Rue Henri Maus
1000 Brussels
tel: +32 (0)2 511 8789

Greenwich
7 rue des Chartreux
1000 Brussels
tel: +32 (0)2 511 4167

Germany

Augustinerkeller
Arnulfstrasse 52
Ecke Zirkus-Krone-Strasse
80335 Munich
tel: +49 (0)89 594 393
www.augustinerkeller.de

Chinesischer Turm
Englischer Garten 3
80538 Munich
tel: +49 (0)89 383 8730
www.chinaturm.de

Königlicher Hirschgarten
Hirschgarten 1
80639 Munich
tel: +49 (0)89 172 591
www.hirschgarten.de

Löwenbräukeller
Nymphenburger Strasse 2
Am Stiglmaierplatz
80335 Munich
tel: +49 (0)89 526 021
www.loewenbraeukeller.com

Paulaner Bräuhaus
Kapuzinerplatz 5
80337 Munich
tel: +49 (0)89 544 6110
www.paulanerbraeuhaus.de

Seehaus im Englischen Garten
Kleinhesselohe 3
80802 Munich
tel: +49 (0)89 381 6130
www.kuffler-gastronomie.de

Viktualienmarkt
Am Viktualienmarkt 6
80331 Munich
tel: +49 (0)89 297 545
www.biergarten-viktualienmarkt.de

Ireland

Davy Byrnes
21 Duke Street
Dublin 2
tel: +353 (0)1 677 5217
www.davybyrnes.com

Guinness Storehouse
St James's Gate
Dublin 8
tel: +353 (0)1 408 4800
www.guinness-storehouse.com

New Zealand

Galbraith's Alehouse
2 Mount Eden Road
Mount Eden
Auckland 1030
tel: +64 (0)9 379 3557
www.alehouse.co.nz

USA

Gordon Biersch Atlanta
848 Peachtree Street NE
Atlanta
GA 30308
tel: +1 404 870 0805
www.gordonbiersch.com

Gordon Biersch Las Vegas
3987 Paradise Road
Las Vegas
NV 89109
tel: +1 702 312 5247
www.gordonbiersch.com

**Gordon Biersch
San Francisco**
2 Harrison Street
San Francisco
CA 94105
tel: +1 415 243 8246
www.gordonbiersch.com

Gordon Biersch San Jose
33 East San Fernando Street
San Jose
CA 95113
tel: +1 408 294 6785
www.gordonbiersch.com

Gordon Biersch Seattle
600 Pine Street
4th Floor, Pacific Place
Seattle
WA 98101
tel: +1 206 405 4205
www.gordonbiersch.com

The Designers

Allied Architecture & Design
43 Dore Street
San Francisco
CA 94103
USA
tel: +1 415 551 2250
www.alliedx.com

Andy Martin Associates
8a All Saints Road
London W11 1HH
UK
tel: +44 (0)20 7229 2425
www.andymartinassociates.com

Arc Design Associates
51–55 Fowler Road
Hainault
Essex IG6 3XE
UK
tel: +44 (0)20 8559 8666

Architecture & Light
60 Brady Street
San Francisco
CA 94103
USA
tel: +1 (415) 676 3999
www.architectureandlight.com

Cantrell & Crowley
Priory
Stillorgan Road
Blackrock
County Dublin
Ireland
tel: +353 (0)1 283 2055
www.cantrellcrowley.com

CYMK Architecture & Design
3 Varden Street
Whitechapel
London E1 2AW
UK
tel: +44 (0)20 7790 7919
www.cymk.co.uk

designLSM
The Bath House
58 Livingstone Road
Hove
East Sussex BN3 3WL
UK
tel: +44 (0)1273 820 033
www.designlsm.com

Gartner Trovato Architects
9 Bungan Street
Mona Vale
NSW 1660
Australia
tel: +61 (0)2 9979 4411

Harrison Ince
2 Jordan Street
Knott Mill
Manchester M15 4PY
UK
tel: +44 (0)161 236 3650
www.harrison-ince.co.uk

Imagination Ltd
25 Store Street
South Crescent
London WC1E 7BL
UK
tel: +44 (0)20 7323 3300
www.imagination.com

Inspire Design Company
49 The Tannery
Lawrence Street
York YO10 3WH
UK
tel: +44 (0)1904 611 091
www.inspired.co.uk

Landini Associates
42 Davies Street
Surry Hills
NSW 2010
Australia
tel: +61 (0)2 9360 3899
www.landini.com.au

Lawrence Beckingham Field
The Sail Loft
1 Limehouse Court
3–11 Dod Street
London E14 7EQ
UK
tel: +44 (0)20 7536 2100

Lex Carter CMA Pty Ltd
Level 3, 56–58 Claremont St
South Yarra
Victoria 3141
Australia
tel: +61 (0)3 9826 8488

Neil Bardrick Associates
Elmbank
60 Camden Park Road
Chislehurst
Kent BR7 5HF
UK
tel: +44 (0)20 8295 0266

r3architects
The Old Town Hall
105 High Street
Rickmansworth
Hertfordshire WD3 1AN
UK
tel: +44 (0)1923 896 178
www.r3architects.com

RKD Architects
59 Northumberland Road
Dublin 4
Ireland
tel: +353 (0)1 668 1055
www.rkd.ie

Ron McCulloch
101 Cockle Bay Wharf
Darling Park
Sydney
NSW 2000
Australia
tel: +61 (0)418 181 813
email: ron@bigbeat.com

Shepherd Neame
17 Court Street
Faversham
Kent ME13 7AX
UK
tel: +44 (0)1795 532 206
www.shepherd-neame.co.uk

SJB Interiors
The Cannery
28 Richards Avenue
Surry Hills
Sydney
NSW 2010
tel: +61 (02) 9380 9911
www.sjb.com.au

Trapp Associates
239 Canyon Boulevard
Suite B
Boulder
CO 80302
USA
tel: +1 (303) 415 0036
www.trappassociates.com

Tuffin Ferraby Taylor
Friary Court
13–21 High Street
Guildford
Surrey GU1 3DG
UK
tel: +44 (0)1483 306 868
www.tftconsultants.com

The Photographers

JD Wetherspoon pubs –
**Briar Rose, The Groves
Company Inn, Metropolitan
Bar, West Kirk, White Swan**

Camera and Design
London
UK
tel: +44 (0)771 1020 5535
www.cameraanddesign.co.uk

Newport Arms Hotel

Paul Gosney
Balmain
Sydney
NSW
Australia
tel: + 61 (0)2 9555 1522
www.paulgosney.com

Cruise Bar

Ross Honeysett
Sydney
NSW 2011
Australia
tel: +61 (0)2 9331 3650
www.rosshoneysett.com

**A la Mort Subite,
L'Archiduc, De Ultieme
Hallucinatie, Falstaff,
Greenwich, Black Friar,
Black Lion, The Counting
House, The County Arms,
Manor Farm Barn, The
Salisbury, Sun Inn,
Warrington Hotel**

Robert Howard
London, UK
tel: +44 (0)7769 975 677
www.robert-howard.co.uk

**The Catcher in the Rye,
Salt House**

Greg Humphrey
Maidstone
Kent
UK
tel: +44 (0)7740 456 656
www.ghponline.co.uk

Mash

Richard Leeney
London
UK
tel: +44 (0)7860 507 555

Galbraith's Alehouse

Geoff Mason
Mount Maunganui
New Zealand
tel: +64 (0)27 494 3554
mason@pl.net

**Café Royal, Crown Liquor
Saloon, Davy Byrnes, The
Guildford Arms, Guinness
Storehouse, Löwenbräukeller,
Munich Beer Gardens,
Paulaner Bräuhaus, The
Philharmonic Dining Rooms,
Prince Alfred & Formosa
Dining Room,
The Vines**

Helen Peyton
Skyreholme
North Yorkshire
UK
tel: +44 (0)1756 720 385
helenpeyton@hotmail.com

De Ultieme Hallucinatie

All @ Internet/Johan Seutens
1090 Jette
Belgium
tel: +32 (0)15 340 591
info@aati.be

Woolwich Pier Hotel

Anson Smart
Sydney
NSW
Australia
tel: +61 (0)2 9699 4122

The Harrow

Stuart Thomas
Gravesend
Kent
UK
tel: +44 (0)7973 192 498
www.stuthomas.com

The Bell, Drift

Mark Townsend
Coventry
West Midlands
UK
tel: +44 (0)2476 461 180
eventz.photography@tesco.net

The Colombian Hotel

Jonny Valian
Sydney
NSW
Australia
tel: +61 (0)2 9310 7466

JD Wetherspoon pubs –
**Lime Kiln, Turls Green,
Winter Gardens**

David Webb Photography
Cramlington
Northumberland
UK
tel: +44 (0)1670 735 333
davidwebb@webbphotos.fsnet.co.uk

Bibliography

Books

Brandwood, Geoff, Davison, Andrew and Slaughter, Michael. *Licensed To Sell*, English Heritage, London, 2004

Bruning, Ted. *Historic Pubs of London,* Prion Books Ltd, London, 2000

Bruning, Ted. *London by Pub: Pub Walks Around Historic London*, Prion Books Ltd, London, 2001

Harden's Bars and Pubs – London, Harden's Ltd, London, 2003

Haydon, Peter. *The English Pub: A History,* Robert Hale Ltd, London, 1994

Websites

American Brewery History
www.beerhistory.com

Beer Advocate
www.beeradvocate.com

Beer Church
www.beerchurch.com

Campaign for Real Ale
www.camra.org.uk

Beer-pages
www.beer-pages.com

WITHDRAWAL

7
1-13

Indianapolis
Marion County
Public Library

Renew by Phone
269-5222

Renew on the Web
www.imcpl.org

For General Library Information
please call 269-1700